To Melissa & Kele
With Gur [signature]

KNUCKLE DRAGGER

[signature]

Ars Longa, Vita Brevis...

KNUCKLE DRAGGER

Robert Sharkey

Copyright © 2019 Robert Sharkey

All rights reserved.

ISBN: 9781091364356

DEDICATION

To Jody, Madeline, Wyatt, Walker and Abigail, for making me feel like a rock star every single day. I love you.

TABLE OF CONTENTS

CHAPTER 1: PUSHUPS 1
CHAPTER 2: THE CALLING 9
CHAPTER 3: REVEILLE 15
CHAPTER 4: OPTIONS 25
CHAPTER 5: ROOK 31
CHAPTER 6: TRYOUTS 43
CHAPTER 7: PTM 53
CHAPTER 8: GUITAR SOLO 59
CHAPTER 9: SERT ACADEMY 67
CHAPTER 10: FEEDING THE DOG 77
CHAPTER 11: TIER COP 87
CHAPTER 12: BLINDSIDED 95
CHAPTER 13: THE CHAIR 103
CHAPTER 14: AMAZING GRACE 109
CHAPTER 15: THE ROAD LESS TRAVELED 115
CHAPTER 16: GRUMPY 121
CHAPTER 17: MAKING A DIFFERENCE 127
CHAPTER 18: NEMESIS 135
CHAPTER 19: OLD SCHOOL 143
EPILOGUE 149

CHAPTER 1: PUSHUPS

The inmates look like scattered blue dots on the three large prison yards below. They seem to be going about their day, peacefully passing time. The atmosphere looks calm and untroubled. If it weren't for the cement walls, concertina wire and armed towers, the place would feel more campus-like than prison-like. From up here on the hilltop, things look peaceful, but tranquility is often very illusive here. What you see on the surface does not reflect what is really going on within. There is always tension, even when you cannot see it, like fissures of a volcano working their way to the surface. Looking out beyond the prison, I notice the beautiful tree-lined hills that surround us. As I take in the contrasting view of prison walls and oak trees, I am reminded of the dichotomy that exists here on so many levels.

When you drive along the highway and notice a prison in the distance, it's pretty easy to tell what it is. They all have that look; the look of a place you don't want to be inside. So why in the world would anyone choose to work there? I hope this book will answer that question, for no better reason than to somehow make sense of it to myself. When you give up loftier, happier ambitions for a job in a place where normal people would not want to be, you can't help but wonder if you've made the right choice.

The gravel road that winds its way to the top of the hill stops at three large water towers that seem to stand guard over the prison. We often run along the gravel road to the water towers, because the view puts everything in perspective. The contrast between the prison walls and the rolling oaks has a way of giving order to things in your own life.

After muscling through enough pushups to make our arms wobbly, we start doing burpees. Then dive bombers. Then mountain climbers. Then we start the whole thing over again. I try to fight back any sign of fatigue as I muscle through each exercise with them. When they start falling out of rhythm with each other, I bark at them to stop counting out loud, because it is messing everyone up. Just shut up and push harder.

I notice that their T-shirts are soaked with sweat. I don't want to kill them with exercises, but I want them to think I'm trying to. I often wonder why I am so hard on them, but I know testing their mettle is an important part of the process. The truth is, I hate being so hard on them. I don't enjoy being such an asshole. Unfortunately, being an asshole is something that has become easier for me through the years. It's not too hard to be such a pain in the ass, because now I don't really know any other way to be. It's just one more gift from the job I'm not particularly proud of at times.

I wanted them to work harder than they had ever worked before, because there was a reward hidden in all of this. If they didn't really want to be here, they could go back to being a regular prison guard. Excuse me, I meant *correctional officer*. A lot of correctional officers get offended if you call them guards. It never mattered to me. In fact, I actually like the term prison guard. It sounds old school. I like old school.

Regardless of whether you saw yourself as a correctional officer or a prison guard, there was something we all wanted from this career: to be more than just one more correctional officer who pounded a tier. That's why we were up on that hill.

Anyone who ever chose this profession had other options in their life. Before taking the job, you must consider the gory details of stabbings, shankings, beatings, rapes and other violent craziness, yet we chose this career path anyway, and then went about developing our own individual storyline. As different as those stories end up being be for each of us, the one thing we have in common is that at some point, we found out that dealing with inmates is not the hardest part of the job. Dealing with everything else that comes with the job is.

We stand up from the pushup position and all take a moment to look out over the horizon. I wonder what makes this prison different from any other. There are thousands of state and federal prisons across the United States, including county jails, juvenile centers, and other detention units. Am I foolish to think I am somehow making some kind of a difference here?

Before I took this job, I never realized how horrific and appalling people could be and what kind of terrible crimes they were capable of. Watching it on the news is one thing. Looking into their eyes is another.

When you find yourself locked behind walls with so much evil, you quickly find out there is a violent nature in society that will never be extinguished. It makes you cynical, because you realize humans are crazy. Even after they are locked up in prison, the absurdity of their behavior continues – stabbings, beatings and riots become daily occurrences. It happens right out in daylight on the yard, for everyone to see. It also happens in the blind spots – in the cells, under the stairwells or behind the handball walls, where nobody can see. It is a volatile world occasionally held together by a shred of necessity to maintain order, until all hell breaks loose again. I can't imagine spending time in that kind of place is any good for you. Can you ever go back to being normal? Someday, I hope to find out.

It doesn't matter if you're a correctional officer, counselor, teacher, nurse, doctor, or any one of the many classifications that work in the prison system; nobody is exempt from bad things happening to them. Since officers spend the most time around inmates, they are attacked more often than anyone else. While some attacks are pre-planned, the majority of them are random and make no sense.

Every day, it seems, we read in the departmental newsletter about another attack on an officer at one of our state prisons. It usually involves somebody who was simply doing their job that day. Some attacks even happen during riots out on the yard, where inmates start by fighting each other in mass, and then turn against officers as they respond to help. Sometimes, it sends numerous officers to the hospital at the same time. For helping. Who would work in that kind of place?

Aside from attacks, there are also hostage takings, many more than the public realizes. At California State Prison, Sacramento, an officer was taken hostage after a violent inmate became upset over a classification committee action against him. To retaliate, he went into the dining room area and grabbed hold of a female officer who was assigned there, and he placed an inmate-manufactured knife, aka *shank*, to her throat. He told everyone to stay back or he would kill her.

After barricading himself with her in a small dining room office, he forced her to remove her stab-proof vest so that he could put it on for his own protection. He took her pepper spray and baton, then he covered the windows so nobody could see what was going on inside. Fortunately, our department has people trained for those situations, and they got her out unharmed.

There were other hostage takings that occurred within our state prisons that went relatively under-publicized too. Some prison uprisings, like Attika, New Mexico, Lucasville, and the fifteen-day standoff in 2004 at the Arizona State Prison

Complex, Lewis, received some degree of media coverage, but like many prison incidents, I am sure there are horrible details still living behind those walls that we will never know.

And they say dealing with inmates is not the hardest part. Really, who would work in such a place?

I like myself a lot better when I'm not thinking about these things, because they bring out the harsher side of me. I get too intense, too serious, and too grandiose. It wasn't bad enough that I took a job as a correctional officer – I decided to make things even more complicated by becoming That Guy. That Guy is always preaching to everyone about riots, hostage takings and other types of prison violence. That Guy tries to get everyone else to join his cause, where people should strive to be better trained and better prepared. When you step into the role of That Guy, there is satisfaction in seeing people become better at their jobs, but there are consequences that come with that role too.

For one thing, people who do not know you often think you're that kind of person all the time. They don't realize it is just your role – one you are simply trying to fulfill with some degree of integrity. They don't realize there's still another side to you, one that is lighthearted and goofy. It wasn't much fun to be thought of as being so rigid and serious, yet like a self-fulfilling prophesy, I often portrayed the role I was supposed to be filling. The thing is, I never asked for any of that. I just wanted to take pride in the job. But at some point, I realized my responsibility to make people safe had become more important than what someone may have thought about me.

I know I probably could have been more conscious of the look I sometimes had on my face. That could have helped, I'm sure. I once had someone at work tell me I walked around with "focus face," and it looked like I was always thinking too much. They were right, about the thinking too much part, but I hoped when someone tells you that you have "focus face" it doesn't mean you sometimes look like an asshole. It probably does.

There are a lot of books written about how to be a SWAT commander. I think I've read just about all of them. I've also lost track of how many leadership books I've read, whether they were written by Navy SEALS, famous coaches, political figures, business people, and anybody else who decided to write a book about what it takes to lead people. At one point, I was running out to buy every new leadership book that came out so I could read it, highlight it, and then stack it with the others on my nightstand. After a while, they started tipping over.

Each book had great ideas and useful principles, but I eventually realized they were just words in a book, edited and rewritten to sound better before it went to print. In real life, it ain't that easy. In real life, things happen so fast that you don't have the time to research your options. And there isn't a delete button. That means you learn by sticking your neck out, getting out there and giving a shit, then screwing it up and swearing you won't make that mistake again. After enough mistakes start stacking up, you might actually become a decent leader – if you still have the job.

I never wanted any of the drama that came with working in prison. I didn't want to be surrounded by negativity every single day. I didn't want to be that annoying, melodramatic, over-the-top pain in the ass who was always trying to find a deeper meaning in his job. I didn't want to be the one who made his guys run all the way up to the top of the hill, made their arms wobbly with pushups and then made them listen to some long-winded diatribe about believing in a cause. This was not what I had in mind as a young boy when I dreamed about what I'd be when I grew up. I wanted to be a rock star, not a prison guard. Playing the guitar was my first true love. It was my passion – one I would never outgrow.

As the commander of a SWAT team in a prison system, the challenges of my role were complicated. As a correctional officer, you already struggle to find meaning and fulfillment in your job at times. Then, if you decide to apply for special assignments like the SWAT team, it can cause animosity as you realize you are giving so much effort, yet nobody really cares. No matter what you do, correctional officers are not seen as "real cops." They are often pigeonholed as lazy, calloused, and insensitive. This unflattering perception is not only from the media and other law enforcement agencies. Sometimes, correctional officers discover that their own management and administration personnel make the same assumptions of them.

As the team commander, you watch the younger guys go through all this, and you understand how they feel, because you also went through it. You see how much training they do, and the physical workouts they put in, besides all the other things they are doing to make themselves better, including the countless hours of range time they put in so they can meet the standards, which are higher than many other "real" law enforcement agencies set. Even with all that work, the negative stereotypes of their profession remains unchanged. Even when people find out they are on a SWAT team, they tend to downsize it because, after all, they are just prison guards, right? Knuckle draggers. The skills they possess and the missions they train for are hidden from public view, so they never get recognition.

I soon realized that aside from my administrative duties, like keeping track of the budget, the training hours, the expenses, and the team roster, it became extremely important to have aspects of leadership I never read about in the SWAT commander or leadership books stacked on my nightstand. For one thing, I found out I wasn't commanding shit: *I* worked for *them,* not the other way around. The other thing I realized was that I would wear different hats at different times.

Depending on the circumstances, I needed to be a counselor, friend, cheerleader, conscience, brother, father, mentor, teacher and student. Whatever time was left over was spent being their boss, and that was the tough part.

As we ran back down the gravel road to head back to the prison, the sounds of heavy breathing and shoes crunching on the gravel road were all we could hear. It was a pleasant, soothing cadence, and it complemented the scenery around us. On the way down the hill, I caught myself thinking about how much I loved and hated my job at the same time. I wondered if I would have taken a different direction in life if I had known I'd end up feeling this way. It was a question I'd ask myself so often throughout my career.

CHAPTER 2: THE CALLING

Growing up, I shared a room with my younger brother, Danny. As the older brother, I took liberties with the room décor. That meant poor Danny had to endure a room peppered with posters and magazine cutouts of 80s rockers, like Mötley Crüe, Ratt, AC/DC and Van Halen. My favorite poster was the concert poster I had over my bed. It was a fold-out that you took out of the Eagles Live album. It showed an overhead shot of one of their massive concerts in a packed stadium. The crowd went from the front of the stage area on the field and filled virtually every seat in the entire stadium. I would often lie back on my bed and look up at that poster and daydream about playing the guitar on stage one day.

My love for music started long before I was putting posters on my wall. Our first house was on the fire station property in the tiny, dusty town of Huron, California. My dad was a firefighter, but he also played in bands on the side. They'd pull the firetrucks out of the large firetruck bay to set up the band instruments inside.

One day, which would be a day I would never forget, they let me stand up in front of a mic stand as the band played a song. I jumped up there without hesitation and yelled some kind of lyrics up towards the microphone with my little acoustic guitar draped around my neck. From that point on, my passion for playing music only got stronger throughout my life. The love of music might be thought of as a good thing, but to me it often felt more like a curse, because it was the source of so many internal conflicts. I wanted to follow this calling, but I would always feel pressure to do the responsible thing and find a career.

My dad started giving me guitar lessons around the time I turned eight. He taught me how to read the little chord drawings in music books and how to actually play and sing songs. I remember how impossible it seemed to get my small fingers to move to where they were supposed to go, but I loved sitting with my dad playing songs. We'd sit there and play along to a music book sitting between us, and that was my introduction to a type of music that was built upon true songwriting, like The Eagles, James Taylor and Jim Croce.

Up on the shelf in the hallway closet was where I truly received my initial education in music. Up on that shelf was where my dad's awesome record collection was to be found: colorful records spanning across the shelf from one side of the closet all the way to the other. I'd have to go to the kitchen to get a chair so I could stand on it to reach the records. I couldn't even estimate how many hours I spent listening to them. While some kids played outside, I would sit there all day, listening to The Eagles, Fleetwood Mac, Styx, Bachman Turner Overdrive, Supertramp, The Outlaws, or anything else he had with a cool looking album cover.

In 7th grade, someone at school introduced me to AC/DC, which pretty much blew my mind. I was like, *where has this been?* Listening to it invoked a different kind of feeling. It was aggressive, but also fun. And that Angus Young guitar playing? It was raunchier than anything I'd ever heard. It made you want to bounce your head up and down to it.

Not long after that, I bought the new *Shout at the Devil* album by Mötley Crüe. I found out, contrary to what some of my friends' parents thought, it really had nothing to do with devil worshipping. Then, a year or two later, one of our friends came over and loaned me a cassette tape with a picture on the front of a little angel-baby smoking a cigarette. I still vividly remember the first time I popped in what was the newly released *1984* album by Van Halen. My life would never be the same again.

Once I bought my first electric guitar and amplifier, I became obsessed. I would play eight hours a day, and sometimes more. That is why I was so skinny: I would rather play the guitar than eat. I'd spend hours and hours practicing all my scales, arpeggios, chord voicings and tried to learn every song I could. I even began writing what I must admit was a lot of really bad music.

Some of the songs may have actually been quite bearable until I started adding lyrics. I'd sit down, enthusiastic about putting pen to paper and creating a song that would someday be heard on the radio, and then, as the ink on the paper formed into lyrics, I'd see "riding down that track" or "takin' the train out of [insert town name here]" or "when I heard that whistle bloooooow" or some other train song. I don't know where this was coming from, but maybe growing up in a neighborhood that was near some train tracks had something to do with it. It was driving me crazy. I knew the world already had enough train-riding songs. It didn't need one more.

When you hear someone play the guitar, it only takes a few notes before you can tell if they have whatever it is that separates great guitarists from good guitarists, and I wanted to be a great guitarist more than anything else in the world. I had a lot of friends who went through their "wanting to play the guitar" phase, and I couldn't help but notice that their guitars usually ended up sitting somewhere in their closet. I never got tired of playing, and I couldn't imagine my guitar in the back of a closet, covered in jackets.

I am very proud that I was learning to play the guitar in the 80s. After all, the music of the 80s was one long guitar solo. Guitar solos started the songs, they ended the songs, and then they filled every conceivable space in between – the vocals were just invasive interruptions. It was a great time to be a guitarist, because there was no such thing as too much guitar. So, I constantly worked on my "chops," because the more "chops" you had, the better. I literally wore out cassette tapes, rewinding them back and forth, just to learn the riffs I was hearing.

I also started taking guitar lessons from some long-haired rocker dude in Fresno. He was in a popular rock band in the area, and he was living the life I wished I could live one day. His band performed in bars and clubs every week, and he had really cool long hair. I couldn't get my hair passed the mullet stage. Party in the back, dude.

In college, I majored in psychology but threw in music classes anywhere they would fit in the schedule, because having lessons with the long-haired rocker dude wasn't enough. I also started learning a lot about music theory. As people began noticing that I was getting really good, I couldn't ignore the obvious question in my life. *Should I go for this?*

The problem with "going for it" as a rock guitarist, especially if you wanted to make it in a famous band, was the way you had to go about doing it, especially back then. If you wanted to make it as a rock guitarist, you had to move to a city that was known for having a music scene. In California, the Bay Area was known to have one, but no place on earth had a bigger, crazier rock scene than Los Angeles, especially the Hollywood area. That was where it was all happening and where aspiring rockers could go to find like-minded musicians.

If you wanted to make it big, at least from the stories I read in Hit Parader and Circus magazine, you had to give up everything you owned that didn't fit into your beat-up little car, and then go buy some rocker clothes at a pawn shop. If you didn't have a car, you could take a train, and then you'd actually have a legit reason to write a train-ride song.

Once you arrived in Los Angeles, you had to live on someone's couch for a while, and then you found some friends to form a band with. Since it's Los Angeles, and it's in the 80s, smack dab in the middle of the hair band movement, eye liner and tights would be necessary accoutrements.

 Once you had a band, you came up with a band name that consisted of two words that may or may not have anything to do with each other. Then you started writing music. Your songs would be about partying and nothing too serious, but you also had to write one ballad on the piano. It should end up as the last song on your album, on Side B.

Once you wrote your ballad, you had to go buy a fog machine. Then, you began taking heroin. Scantly-dressed groupies will want you, and through it all, you can hope to avoid drug addition, crabs, herpes, gonorrhea and unexpected fatherhood. Then, you wrote a book if you lived that long. Maybe at some point you give it all up to become a banker or a car salesman, or hell, maybe even a prison guard. This was how getting famous went down, I was absolutely sure of it. After all, I read the articles. I was willing to give it a shot, except for the taking heroin part.

Okay, to be completely honest, I didn't want to wear ripped-up tights or eye-liner either. I didn't even know how I would go about moving to Los Angeles, because the money I was making at Round Table Pizza was barely enough pocket money to buy Taco Bell, much less to relocate to LA. Besides, I had terrible hair. Considering all the things you had to do to become a rock star, I really hoped I'd outgrow my passion so that I could figure out what I really wanted to do with my life.

It never happened. I didn't become a rock star, because I never took a plane, a train or a car to Los Angeles to chase the dream. I never had groupies, and I never tried heroin. I became a prison guard instead. Oh, excuse me. I meant to say, "correctional officer."

CHAPTER 3: REVEILLE

Joining the Army right out of high school was the only way I was going to be able to afford to go to college. It was also a great way to break away from my small home town, where I felt I had limited opportunities to figure out what I wanted to do with my life. I hoped that by the time I got out of the Army, then went to college, I'd somehow know what I was supposed to do with my life.

When I graduated basic training, I received orders to report to my regular unit at the 25th Infantry Division, Hawaii. Yeah, I know, terrible, right? When I showed up at Bravo Company, 1st Battalion/ 14th Infantry, I was the youngest, skinniest, pimpliest person in the entire company, and I would remain the youngest, skinniest, pimpliest person for quite a while. When I walked up to the front desk to check in, I probably looked like quite a sight pulling my bags, guitar case and amplifier up the walkway. After walking up to the CQ desk (short for "charge of quarters," which was the soldier assigned to guard the front entrance to the barracks), the sergeant there told me to go inside and wait at the end of the hallway to meet the first sergeant. Hey, that's nice, I thought. He probably wants to welcome me aboard.

I went in and headed down the long hallway just like I was told, and the first thing I noticed was that the floors were polished like glass, so I did what I could to avoid dragging my stuff on the floor. Once I reached the end of the hallway, I set everything down and assumed the position of parade rest, just like a good little soldier. In this position, you're supposed to have your eyes locked straight ahead, but I couldn't help but stare up above the doorway, where two huge crisscrossed muskets were hand-painted into the wall, the insignia of the United States Infantry.

* * *

When I told my dad I was joining the Army, he said, "Hey, that's great! Just make sure you join anything but the Infantry." I figured that was good advice, because infantry guys are the ones who spend time crawling around in the muck. I was okay with not having to crawl around in the muck, so my plan was to follow his advice.

I reported to the Military Entrance Processing Station (MEPS) to choose my MOS (Military Operational Specialty), the coding system for every military job. When they called me into one of the offices, I walked in and said, "I'll take anything but the infantry."

The sergeant at the desk laughed and said there were a lot of really great jobs that weren't infantry, and he proceeded to show me videos of different MOSs. Every video looked like some strange propaganda: bad acting soldiers with fake smiles walked around zombie-like, performing their duties as though they actually enjoyed placing boxes of stuff on shelves or taking big wheels off of trucks.

I was getting tired of watching videos, until he put in the video for infantry. It was the only one in which the soldiers didn't seem to be pretending to like their jobs: they actually looked like they were having fun. Moments later, I walked out of the MEPS station with my orders in my hand, and I kept reading the top line over and over, just to make sure it said what I thought it said. *11B INFANTRY*. I wondered what the hell I had just done.

* * *

I thought that after getting through basic training things would get easy at my regular unit. Plus, it was HAWAII! I figured after the first sergeant introduced himself to me, maybe I could get a head start on in-processing, I could go check in, get my key to my room, and then go find a beach. What I did not anticipate was that I was about to meet the meanest human being I'd ever met in my life.

When First Sergeant Stanley rounded the corner, the look on his face was, without a doubt, the most cantankerous expression on a human face I'd ever seen. When he saw me waiting for him, his expression only got worse. As he glared at me, it looked like he was imagining what it might feel like to kill me with his bare hands. I immediately thought *uh-oh*, as he came in closer for a better look. He seemed to be thinking, *Just what in the FUCK is this standing here in my hallway?*

He didn't give me a handshake. He didn't say hello. He didn't utter any welcoming words at all, at least not the type of words normal people give to other normal people when they first greet each other. His way of welcoming me aboard was to look down at my guitar case and then back up into my eyes.

"You have GOT to be *fucking kidding me*. You *maggot*."

The "maggot" part grumbled deep and disdainful, almost demonic. I then saw the patches on his BDUs, like the Combat Infantryman Badge, jump wings, air assault, and his Ranger tab over his 25th Infantry Division Tropic Lightning patch, or "electric strawberry" as we called it. As he turned to walk into his office, I noticed the combat unit patch on his right shoulder was the 1st Infantry patch, or the Big Red 1. That was who he served with in Vietnam.

It was 1985, so there were still quite a few Vietnam vets left in the military. Some of those guys had not even reached twenty years of service yet. We had a few Vietnam vets in our company, including my squad leader, Staff Sergeant Rivera, who was a pathfinder during the war. One of the E-7s in our company had scars all over his face and a metal plate in his leg from the war. He was really quiet and really scary, so nobody ever asked him about it. The thing I remember more than anything else about those Vietnam vets in our company was they did not fuck around. Not one bit. I learned to love that about them.

First Sergeant Stanley would end up making every drill sergeant I ever met in basic training look like a Boy Scout. He wasn't your friend. He wasn't your buddy. He wasn't going to give one shit about your self-esteem or how you felt about yourself. His job was to train you so you could stay alive. Much more importantly though, he taught you to never, ever give up on your partners. Even years later, I would expect the guys on our SWAT team to have each other's backs, and he was the reason why I had a problem with anyone who didn't.

One night, First Sergeant Stanley pulled the whole company out into the middle of the quad at 0230 hours, because one of our guys ended up in the hospital with a broken jaw from a fistfight in town. He told us the next time one of his troops came back beaten up, he'd better see a whole bunch of his troops coming back beaten up. He then proceeded to PT us until we could barely stand (I guess that was where I learned to do that).

He was one mean son of a bitch, but we would have done anything for that man, because we knew he always had our backs. As we could see through his harshness after a while, even his favorite name for everyone, "maggot," became a term of endearment. I know there was a piece of him that always stayed with me, especially when I had to be responsible for my own guys years later.

I loved the infantry because it taught me so much about myself. Basic training was a cakewalk compared to some of the things we had to do, like navigating up and down the steep forested gulches of Hawaii. I found out the term "light infantry" was actually a cruel joke. Light infantry sounds like a nice thing, but it is just another way of saying *supported by your spine.* Our rucksacks were so full of junk that I had to place my ruck on the ground and literally crawl into the shoulder straps. Once I had my arms in the straps, I'd roll over to my hands and knees and work myself up to a standing position. I would practically tip over like a drunk sailor until I got my bearing, and then, before you knew it, we had covered miles and miles of up and down terrain without one single thought of ever quitting.

When you're new to an infantry unit, your job back then was to keep your mouth shut until you earned everyone's trust. You got messed with a lot as a newbie, and you had to put up with it. Most of it was good-natured, but when it came to Private First Class Bowman, it wasn't.

PFC Bowman did everything he could to make my life miserable right from the start. His cigarette would dangle up and down from the corner of his mouth as he berated me any chance he had. He called me every name in the book and harassed me at every opportunity. As a skinny, pimple-faced, quiet kid who was still unsure of himself, I didn't want to make things worse. I admit it though, I seriously started to hate him.

At the time, I was the newest guy in the whole company, so I figured this was what happened to you, especially since nobody said a word about it. That is, until Specialist (E-4) Brian Sells decided to put an end to it. As far as he was concerned, this shit had gone on far too long. He decided to stop by my room one night, and what he said changed my life.

I was sitting on my bunk, spit-shining my boots when he walked in.

"Do you realize you are serving the best country in the entire world?" Sells asked me.

I wasn't sure what to say. I put everything down on the bed and just listened. Brian Sells was someone I looked up to. He had a confident yet cheerful way about him and was always smiling like nothing ever bothered him. He was a bit older, and he had a lot of experience, including some great stories about Panama, Korea, Japan, Australia, and about his time in Ranger School. He kind of took me under his wing when I got there and showed me the ropes, like where to go and not go on the island. He showed me uniform tricks like the best way to starch your BDUs so they were like cardboard, and how to spit-shine your jump boots and finish with Mop & Glo without making them look like Mop & Glo, and also how to get that pain in the ass outer coating off our Class A insignia so it shined like a mirror.

"No, I don't think you do," he answered himself, proving it was really more of a statement than a question. "Here's the thing. If you actually knew you were serving the best country in the world, you would be walking around with some pride in yourself. Since you aren't walking around with some pride in yourself, that means you don't realize that you're serving the best country in the world."

I was about to say something, then I closed my mouth. Don't say anything. Shut your mouth and listen.

"You don't believe in yourself. You know it, I know it. Everyone around here knows it. I've watched you walk to chow. I've watched you walk out to the PX. I've seen it in your body language, walking around all slouched over with your head down. Here you are, serving your country, and you don't even realize how good it feels, because you're letting someone like Bowman mess with you every single day. Until you do something about it, it is *never* going to stop. If you think Bowman is the last of it, you're gonna have a life of that kind of thing. Don't be the guy people think they can fuck with. Believe in your heart that you are just as good as any other man here, and it will come true. But as long as you let someone like Bowman do this to you, pride will be a feeling you will never get to know. How long you gonna live this way?"

With that, he walked out and slammed the door, leaving me with a lot to think about.

The next morning after PT, I went back to my room in the barracks for a minute and walked over to look out the back window. On the street behind the quad, I saw our little PX, and I was sure that was the one Sells saw me walking out to, all slouched over. What a joke I am, I thought.

I looked around the base, and I saw soldiers in uniform walking around and formations of troops running along the roadways. They looked so proud and confident. I looked across the way, and I could see the massive American flag down by the entrance gate flapping in the wind. I thought to myself, of all the flags I've ever seen, I am looking at the most beautiful flag in the world, the American flag, flying proudly on an American military base – and this was certainly no ordinary military base.

I thought back to the black and white photos I saw on the walls of our battalion headquarters. Along those hallway walls, there were photos of all the current and past leadership at Schofield Barracks, some Vietnam photos involving the 25th Infantry Division, and, shockingly to me, photos of the aftermath of December 7, 1941, when, on the day of Pearl Harbor, Japanese aircraft flew over Schofield Barracks and fired upon the same quads we were living in.

I thought about what it must have felt like to have enemy planes flying directly overhead, right there on American soil. I suddenly felt very proud to serve my country, because I realized it was not something everyone got to do. I was also very proud to be in the infantry, because we were working harder than anyone else around us. I told myself that I owed myself more credit and more respect than I was giving myself. And, I didn't want to be the guy people could pick on. No. Fuck that.

* * *

I had been in a few fistfights in my life, but I am not a fighter. It was just something that happened where I grew up, and even though most fights ended up as wrestling matches in the dirt, I lost a lot more fights than I had won. Truth be told, I'm not sure I won any of them. Even though I had planned to stand up to Bowman if he harassed me again, it was hard to not think about the last fight I got into in high school.

It was the morning before school started, and I conducted one last rehearsal in the mirror before heading out to the bus stop. I practiced my technique, just to make sure I had it down. My plan was to smash this other kid in the face with my backpack of books when I saw him at the school bus drop-off area. He had been picking a fight with me every single day, and I decided I'd go ahead and put a stop to it. He was a lot bigger than me, but my secret weapon was the six months of Tae Kwon Do I had been taking. I figured after I whacked him in the head with my books, I'd be able to tee off on him with some Tae Kwon Do moves. I almost felt sorry for him for the damage I was about to do.

Just as I predicted, he was right there waiting for me at the bus area at school. He immediately started in on me by walking up and blocking my path. As soon as he went into his morning ritual with me, I wasted no time at all, and just swung away. *And it's a swing and a miss, folks, Strike Threeeeee.*

I completely whiffed. I swung so wildly that he just jumped out of the way. If the wall behind him had a nose, I would have bloodied it for sure. He was so big and fat that I was shocked that I missed. Then I got to find out that the kind of Tae Kwon Do I was taking wasn't the kind of Tae Kwon Do that taught you how to beat up a bully. It was also not the kind that helped when someone outweighing you by a hundred pounds sits on top of you and punches you in the face, over and over and over as approximately two-thirds of your high school watches in horror.

* * *

With that on my mind, I headed to the latrine. It was our squad's turn to clean it, which meant I'd see Bowman there. As I walked through the latrine doors, I saw him with his customary cigarette dangling from his mouth. He snickered and walked straight at me. I tried to avoid him by diverting over to the rolls of toilet paper and then heading over to the stalls. As I was standing in one of the stalls changing out empty rolls, he walked up close, and he just stood there, right behind me. I tried to ignore him, and the silence was eventually broken by his obnoxious giggling.

"Change that shit paper, you fucking *newbie*. That's all you're good for anyway. Shit paper."

I leaned back into him to nudge him off me, since he was practically in the stall with me. When I nudged him, he pushed me. Then I snapped. As I spun, he jumped back and I came out of the stall at him. As he put his hands up, I swung. I didn't miss this time, unlike the bus drop-off area in High School. His eyes bulged out wide with shock when I came after him.

When I hit him in the mouth, his cigarette exploded into pieces, and sparks flew all over the place like fireworks. As the entire squad stopped what they were doing to watch us, Sells reached over and shut the latrine doors so nobody else could walk in. *This ends. Right now.*

Word got out regarding what had happened, and just like that, I was no longer the new guy. I also suddenly found out I had more friends than I knew what to do with. From that point forward, I walked differently, talked differently, and acted differently. Not long after that, they moved Bowman and me into the same room together, and we actually became really close friends. We never once spoke of the incident, though.

CHAPTER 4: OPTIONS

When my enlistment time was up, I did everything I could to ignore any notion I had about reenlisting. I loved the Army, but it was time to get out to see what life had in store for me.

As I walked around one last time to say goodbye to everyone, it was hard to not get a little choked up. After all, my life changed so much because of my time in the Army, and all those guys had become my best friends. I also had the amazing experience of deploying to different countries, like Japan and Korea, where I not only found out about different cultures and ways of life, but I got a chance to realize just how far the world stretches beyond what we call home. I would never again be the same, and the confidence and pride I developed from my experiences there were something nobody could ever take away from me.

I wasn't sure what I was going to do with my life, but my reputation at some point became the guy who was supposed to get out of the Army and play music. There wasn't much time in the infantry to play the guitar, but I practiced every chance I had. I think the most important lesson I learned from the military was if you work hard at something, you will get out of it what you put into it. I know that was one of the reasons I continued to become a better guitar player even with minimal practice time, because I only practiced the things that were hard to do.

After saying my goodbyes, as I walked out that last time, Donnell Hughes, a guy from Mississippi, who lived in the room next to me in the barracks, yelled out to me.

"Sharkey, I almost hate to see you go. I was just starting to get to the point where I could stand listening to you play that damned guitar."

That really meant a lot.

* * *

After the Army, I started attending community college. I decided to major in psychology, because there was something about the human mind, especially its learning processes, that I became drawn to. I'm sure a lot of this was because I am, and always have been, a chronic over-thinker. It suited me.

During that time, I played in a few bands here and there, and I joined our jazz ensemble at the community college. I learned a lot from those older, experienced jazz musicians. That was when I learned about staying in the pocket. When it was your moment to shine, do it, but until then don't be an individual. I remember how those guys would shoot you a look if you were doing too much, but they would also reach over and turn up your amp if they couldn't hear your solo.

After graduating community college with an associate's degree in psychology, I transferred to the California State University, Stanislaus. It is often thought of as one of the most boring colleges in the state of California, if not the entire universe, but we did not seem to have a shortage of beer drinking or other indulgences, I would have to say.

I found some buddies to start a band with, and we wrote our own songs and built enough of a cover set list to play at a few parties. Unfortunately, money was an issue because, well, we didn't have any. We were college students, so our music equipment was rather shoddy. Luckily, our lead singer had a credit card. That gave us just enough equipment to entertain the idea of doing great things, but I think we realized our true fate was to get real jobs someday. In the back of our minds, we believed it was possible to make it. When our lead singer moved up to Washington, I ended up taking over the singing duties. However, when it gets to the point that I'm taking over singing duties, we ain't going far.

Playing the guitar sent me into another world, and it only got worse as time went on. I figured my big career decision would come to me at any time, but I just kept waiting and waiting for it. When I had my guitar in my hands, I would escape to another world, and into a place of total creative expression and abandonment – it was extremely addictive, like a drug. I'd lose track of conversations in the room, appointments, and any other commitments I had. Playing the guitar gave me a feeling nothing else could ever imitate. I wanted to quit everything else, and just play the guitar.

I was still wrestling with this dilemma as I graduated and was handed my bachelor's degree. Initially, I had planned to continue studying psychology into graduate school, but I quickly realized how impossible that seemed.

I used up my Army college fund, and the job I had was not making a lot of money, so it was going to be very difficult to afford to continue with an education. At the time, I was working with kids in group homes. I loved the job because it was related to my area of study and because I found out how much I enjoyed being around kids. The situations that contributed to why they were each placed into a group home varied, and although each of their stories was very sad, it was extremely rewarding to be around them.

Although it was my role to help teach the kids lessons about life and how to better socialize with their world, the person who usually learned the most from those lessons was me. Whether it was dealing with a child who is lying on the floor crying insistently because he misses his Mommy (with her picture clutched in his hands), figuring out the best way to deal with candy bar theft from the local 7-11, teaching someone how to thread a worm on a hook, or answering the tough questions that come up as you tuck them into bed for the night, I felt like it was all a great preparation for situations I would later face in life. More than anything else, it taught me that there is nothing in this universe more precious than a child.

I was tired of not having any money or nice things though. I loved working with those kids, but I was *tired* of having to do all my auto repairs myself anytime my car broke down. I actually fantasized about how it must feel to be so successful in life that you could actually drive your car to a shop and drop it off to let *them* figure it out. I felt like that would really be making it.

My dad worked for the California Department of Forestry (which later became CAL FIRE). At that time, he was a firefighter trainer at a state prison, just like his father before him. They were both fire captains who trained inmates to fight fires. In California, the many wildland fires that occur are fought with a multi-agency approach, including the use of thousands of inmate firefighters.

As a result of his job, my dad became friends with a lot of correctional officers. He often tried to sell the correctional officer career to me, saying that it was a good job with good benefits. Anytime he mentioned that I should put in an application with the California Department of Corrections, it seemed like the worst thing I could ever do with my life. Finally, just to appease him and get him to stop bringing it up, I agreed to meet up with one of his friends who worked at the prison.

I drove down to the prison and met his friend out by the entrance building with a flag pole out front. As he escorted me inside, the slam of the large heavy gates closing behind us made me think, *Oh, there's no way in hell.* As it turned out, that feeling wasn't even half as bad as actually walking out onto the prison exercise yard. Who knew that would be the very same yard I would be looking down upon years later as we were doing pushups by the water towers?

My dad's friend was what they call a "correctional counselor," who works with inmate case factors and classification issues. Although they are peace officers, they don't have to walk the tiers like most correctional officers. As we walked and talked, he told me about their pay, their benefits, and, surprisingly, how they actually enjoyed their jobs.

When you are uncomfortable, it's kind of hard to hide it, especially out in the middle of a prison exercise yard. It is something you eventually learn to get over, with experience, but the first time you step out onto a prison yard is a moment you tend to never forget. The inmates can tell right away if you don't belong there, even if most of them could probably care less about you. At that time, I had long hair and as we walked by a group of inmates who were exercising by the culinary building, a couple of them whistled at me.

"Hey, nice hair."

I tried to act as if I hadn't even noticed them, but it would have been impossible not to, especially a group of hard-looking guys staring at you who are covered in tattoos. I was like, *Nah, I'm good.* You'd have to be crazy to work in that kind of place, and I couldn't wait to get the hell out of there.

CHAPTER 5: ROOK

The problem with a bachelor's degree in psychology is that you can't do much with it. You graduate and somehow think you've got humans figured out, and then you don't hesitate to help everyone else out with their problems. You have just enough knowledge to annoy your friends and family. The reality, though, is that you need to get at least a master's degree if you want to work in a related field, and it isn't going to be for as much money as you probably thought, especially when you consider how much it costs to go to graduate school. I had two degrees, with options ahead of me, yet, my dilemma continued. Then a certified letter showed up in the mailbox.

It was from the California Department of Corrections. I suddenly remembered half-heartedly sending in an application. I had no intention of actually going through with it, especially after my visit to the prison. I went ahead and opened the letter, and it said all I had to do was call the number listed and I'd be offered a correctional officer job at one of the California State Prisons. The problem with that was it could have been anywhere in California, since state prisons were located basically from up near Oregon to the Nevada side down to the Mexican border.

I didn't see myself as the correctional officer type. If I became a correctional officer, I'd have to enforce rules and pay attention to shenanigans. I wasn't interested in either. I also feared it was the kind of job that would change me, and I'd have to become a different kind of person. I'd become less carefree and more serious. I'd have to grow a mustache, and wear mirrored sunglasses. I'd have to learn how to make a *bust* and walk up to tattooed dudes working out by the culinary and act like they didn't make me nervous and I knew what they were really up to. I didn't want to make a bust or act like I knew what people were up to. And I definitely didn't want to grow a mustache.

Some gum-popping lady with very little patience answered the phone in Sacramento. I almost hung up. When I reluctantly gave her my name, she told me to hold on while she looked up my information. She said there was an opening at Sierra Conservation Center in Jamestown. The name might sound like a nice place with environmental interests, but it is really just a prison. It is actually the same prison both my dad and grandfather trained inmate firefighters at. I was going to say, "Thank you, but no, thank you," but somehow my voice said yes as my mouth opened.

What the hell did I just do?

I had just officially slammed the door on my dreams of playing music. After all I had been through, what surprised me the most about it was that it actually felt good. A massive weight was suddenly off my chest. Now, I had a direction, and I didn't have to think about what I was going to do anymore. I also wondered if maybe there was a chance a person could go to work in a prison without having to act like a person who works in prison.

Would that be possible?

* * *

The correctional officer academy was part law enforcement, part paramilitary in design. On the one hand, we were going to end up with a badge. That was the law enforcement part. On the other hand, they yelled at you a lot. That was the paramilitary part. When something is advertised as being "paramilitary," you can expect to get into formations and be marched around, and you'll probably have to do PT. We did those things, but it was nowhere near the intensity of what I had experienced in the Army. It was actually a lot of fun, because it was sort of like the military, but not as bad.

Our two primary "drill instructors" wore Smokey the Bear hats, just to make sure everyone understood they were not to be trifled with. It was also quite evident that anyone planning to make fun of them should wait until we got back to the barracks to do so. So, we did.

On the very first day of the academy, they had us in a long processing line that went from the entrance building all the way out to the parking lot. The academy cadre were out there in full force, yelling at people and getting in everyone's face. They'd march up to a random cadet and ask something like "What is your problem, *cadet*?"

I was surprised at how many people couldn't even answer that. Some only stood there, stuttering incoherently. It was obvious the academy cadre were only trying to stress the cadets out, just to see who couldn't take it. It actually worked, because there were a handful of them who picked up their suitcases, walked straight back to their vehicles and drove home. Their careers lasted almost four and a half minutes. I actually enjoyed all the yelling. It reminded me of being back in the Army where getting yelled at was evidence that someone cared about you.

Since I had already been yelled at by the best yellers in the world, it was easy to play along with the game. When they saw I knew how to get everyone into formation and knew how to call cadence, they selected me to be the company commander for Sierra Company. Each of the companies had a cadet commander, which was AKA for: *fellow cadet who has to be in charge of the other cadets and who hopefully doesn't look like a total kiss ass*.

My favorite thing about being the company commander was that I got to call cadence for every PT run. In the Army, running to cadence calls was one of my favorite things. I remembered how some of those sergeants called cadence with such powerful tone and rhythm it made you feel like you could run all day.

The best cadence I ever heard was from Drill Sergeant Kirkendoll back at Fort Benning, Georgia during basic training. He was our senior drill sergeant and he had the deepest, most southern drawl ever. He was one scary dude, who always spoke to us as though we were the vilest of all creatures, but his cadence calls were the best, without exception. You wouldn't have traded being there in that moment for anything else in the world. The way he sounded as his voice echoed along those Fort Benning roadways made you love the Army with every ounce of your soul. He didn't just yell, scream, or bark out a cadence call – he *sang* it, with a type of soul that made you *believe* in what you were singing, as if they were the most important words you've ever uttered in your life.

As each of the companies at our academy ran by the other companies, you could hear their cadence calls. It was always the same *Two ol' ladies were-a lyin' in the bed* or *C-130 rollin' down the sta-RRIP* junk we all remembered from the military. God, I was sick of those. I quickly thought up some new cadence lyrics for us, and I really dug deep when I sang them, thinking back to the styles I had heard from Senior Drill Sergeant Kirkendoll and even mean ol' First Sergeant Stanley. When those men stepped out in front of a formation, you knew they were there.

I loved calling cadences for the same reason I loved playing music. You should find a way to be original and use your own personal voice. That, to me, is what playing the guitar is all about. When I stepped out to call cadence for our company runs, people in the other companies, including their cadre, would look over to see which company sounded like that. When your formation really gets into a cadence call, it has a different kind of sound. It bellows. It feels as if a train is coming.

As the cadet company commander, it was my job to make sure everyone was where they were supposed to be on time and in the proper uniform, whether we were supposed to wear our ugly brown UPS-looking uniforms, PT sweats or running attire. It was my first taste of leadership, which also meant that I was the guy who got his ass chewed if anything went wrong or if we showed up at the wrong location. I realized I actually liked having that kind of responsibility.

On the day of graduation, everyone had their wife, husband, boyfriend or girlfriend ceremoniously pin their badge on for the very first time. During my academy, it was one of those things everyone seemed to talk about: getting their badge pinned on by their special person. My girlfriend showed up for graduation, but in the mass of people I couldn't find her. I looked around and noticed everyone had their badges on their uniforms already, and graduation was about to begin. I figured I'd just pin it on myself, but I realized it was a lot harder than you might think, especially as you're looking upside-down at your badge from above.

After jabbing myself in the finger, another graduate who I didn't even know walked by.

"Hey man, could you help me out a sec?"

"Yeah, I guess. But we gotta be in formation, like right now."

"I need you to pin this on me." I held my hand out with my badge sitting on top of my outstretched palm. He looked at me like he was wondering what kind of idiot couldn't figure out how to pin his own badge on.

"Yeah, I know," I said, "but I can't get the fucking pin inside the little doohickey."

He shook his head a little, and then grabbed my badge and reached over to pin it on my shirt. It took him longer than we both expected, which only made it that much more uncomfortable.

"Thanks... uh, bro," I said after he pinned it on. I figured we were now much closer than unfamiliar passerby.

He gave me a bit of an odd look and turned to walk off as he said, "Sure, no problem, Dude," and I never saw him again.

As it turned out, the momentous occasion of having my badge pinned on for the first time was not really all that incredible.

After graduating and getting sworn in, working in a prison ended up being sometimes better and sometimes worse than I had anticipated. Being the new guy, I often had to work first watch, which was the shift between 2230 and 0630 hours. The nice thing about first watch is that the inmates are sleeping. The bad thing about first watch is that you shouldn't be.

Playing cards was a great way to stay awake, and it gave you a chance to get to know the officers you worked with, especially the older guys who knew some really cool card games. Over countless hands of cards, we'd talk about sports, hobbies or whatever subject came up. I found it interesting that even though many of them had the seniority to work any shift, some of them preferred first watch, because it gave them more time with their family. Some of them, on the other hand, simply hated being around too many people.

Between having to pull CQ duty in the Army and a few other jobs that occasionally involved the night shift, it wasn't the first time I had to work through the night. Staying awake overnight in prison was a little bit different though – there is definitely more motivation to stay awake.

One particular officer I worked with would only get out of his chair when it was time to count the inmates. As soon as we got back to the office, he'd lean back in his chair and say, "Wake me up for the next count, rook." He'd then set his flashlight down, drape one foot over the other on top of the desk and cross his arms in front of his chest. He'd nuzzle his chin down towards his chest like a curled-up puppy. He looked so cozy that I half-imagined that at some point his thumb was going to make its way into his mouth.

It was rough sitting there watching him sleep, because it was making me so drowsy. My skin tingled, my eyes blurred and my mind fogged. I wondered if it would be okay to just close my eyes, maybe just for a moment. Whenever I'd feel my eyes shut, I'd jerk back awake as I imagined some crazed inmate sneaking up on both of us with a rusted shank, trying to escape. Too many prison movies and too many stories from academy sergeants, I know. In reality, it was very quiet, and all the inmates were safely locked away.

One night, the officers told me it was my turn to go around to wake up the early culinary workers. They started in the culinary at 4 am, which meant we had to wake them up during the count. On this particular yard, it was a dormitory setting with 36 inmates per dorm, all sleeping on bunkbeds. During wake-ups, an officer would head off into the dorms ahead of the other officers who were counting everyone. One of the older officers handed me a list of the inmates I was supposed to wake up, and he gave me the only instructions I apparently needed: "Don't let us catch up to you."

With my list in hand, I hustled into each dorm alone and scrambled back and forth across the center isle searching for each inmate on the list. Unfortunately, this was before they painted bunk numbers on the wall above the beds, which meant I woke up a lot of wrong inmates. None of them were happy about this.

One particular inmate wouldn't wake up. He was an enormously large man, whose feet stuck out beyond his blanket and hung off the end of the top bunk. I called his name. Nothing. I called it again, louder. Still, nothing. I whispered, "Waaaaake uuuuuup!" as loud as I could, right into his ear. He didn't budge. I shook a foot. I poked an arm. I jabbed a shoulder. Still nothing.

The officers who were counting came in and walked by me as they silently counted the inmates. The older officer who gave me my directions looked over at me, wondering what the hell I was doing. I held up my hands as if I didn't know what to do and then watched them walk right on by me without any assistance. *Figure it out, rook*.

When I tried to wake the inmate up again, I started making so much noise that several other inmates woke up. It was getting dangerous for me.

"C'mon man!" one said.

"Get your shit together!" another cursed.

"Check your list, dumbass!"

Then, one of the inmates grumbled, "You'd better check his pulse, bro."

My heart stopped. I stared at the large inmate on the bunk and thought, *Oh no, not that. Please, don't be dead.* I gave him one more good shake, hard enough to shake the entire bunk, which woke up the inmate sleeping on the lower bunk. I was really pissing these guys off.

I realized he had to be dead. This was bad. I grabbed the inmate's hand and placed two fingers on his inner wrist to see if I could detect a pulse. We were never really taught how to find a pulse in CPR/First Aid training, but I remembered learning how to do it back in the Boy Scouts. I wanted to be sure he was dead.

No pulse. Nothing.

I moved my fingers around, thinking maybe I was in the wrong spot.

Nothing.

I pressed the button on my radio to contact the sergeant, but I let go of it before the words left my mouth. I thought to myself, before I go broadcasting that kind of radio transmission over the entire prison radio system, I'd better make damn sure this dude was dead. One more check. If the cavalry showed up and this guy was only sleeping, I'd never live it down. I'd be *that guy*. I wondered if maybe I wasn't finding a pulse because he was so fat. I placed two fingers on his neck. Every alive person has a pulse in his carotid. I pressed down.

Nothing.

I pressed harder, pushing my fingers so deep they went into the folds of his neck fat.

Nothing. *Shit!* I moved my fingers to the opposite side of his neck. One last check, and I'm making that call. Then I'll have to start CPR. I ain't doing mouth to mouth though. Not on this dude. No way.

My hands were now pressing into the thick, blubbery folds of his neck when his eyes suddenly popped open. Was I checking his pulse, or choking him? Well, I don't know who flinched more. I think first it was him, then me. I jumped backwards, thinking he was going to kill me.

"What the FUCK are you doing!?"

"I thought you were *dead*! My God! Do you even have a pulse?"

"I'm a deep sleeper, asshole," he responded. "And you need to keep your hands off of motherfuckers!"

I really hate this job. Seriously, who would work in such a place?

* * *

As a new officer, I was hired as Permanent Intermittent Employee (PIE). PIEs existed for one purpose: overtime avoidance. This meant I never knew when I was going to work. Most of the PIEs were on-call, meaning you had to answer your phone to get a shift. They didn't call you unless one of the regulars called in sick and they needed you to fill the vacant position. That meant the watch sergeant had to go all the way through the entire list of PIEs before they would get to your name, because they had to make it fair.

At one point during my PIE tenure, we had over 60 PIEs at our prison. Once in a while, you'd get hard-scheduled into a vacant position for a week or so, but you'd always end up rotating on-call, and your schedule never stayed the same. To me, it was fairly depressing, especially as my inconsistent schedule caused me to fall out of contact with all my college buddies. I could never make plans to do anything, especially on the weekend. Then, even when you were hired for a position, when you were a PIE you could never feel like you were actually part of the team; you were only there for a shift.

I had to be a PIE for three long years. My group remained PIEs longer than any other group ever had to at our prison. Each group of PIEs "rolled over" into full-time positions based upon time in service, the budget, and vacant positions. At the time, it was a combination of bad luck regarding all three of those things for us.

During those years, I missed out on things like weddings, vacations and several get-togethers with my friends, because I'd have to be on-call, and I'd have to work every holiday. Since

PIEs were paid by the hour, if I didn't work, I didn't get paid. I'd often think about my college buddies, and I missed spending time with them. They all still hung out together, playing cards and watching Giants games, while I went to work in prison. When one of them got married, I had to miss the wedding because as a PIE I couldn't get the time off. That was tough for me to miss, and once that happened, I think it was pretty much the final indicator that I had truly gone off in a different direction than the rest of them. That was around the time they stopped contacting me to invite me to stuff, since I couldn't ever make it. It was just one more thing to make me wonder if I had made the right career decision.

The thing I hated most about the job was that there was absolutely no room for individuality or creativeness. We were ridiculously micromanaged and since our department was inundated with lawsuits and court orders, there was a lot of oversight and pressure from management to do things a certain way. It never felt like we could think for ourselves. Individual discretion was frowned upon, and anytime you tried to think outside the box, it felt like an act of futility. I missed the carefree attitude I had before the job. Especially as a guitarist, I saw myself as an artist, and free to do things my way, but that's not how a job in prison works.

In prison, if you fail to enforce certain rules, inmates will take advantage. When inmates take advantage, bad things can happen. If you don't pay attention, you are putting you and your partners at risk. I could feel myself changing because of the job. I began to notice things about people. Prison made me start to hate bullies or anyone who took advantage or preyed on others, even more than I ever did before. Prison is full of such people.

Working in that kind of environment, you quickly realize there are terrible people in the world, worse than you ever imagined. It was troubling to see how many people there are out there who harm children. We knew who they were, because we had to constantly protect them from the rest of the prison population. If you are not careful, being among all these people can make you change your perception of humanity. I didn't like the change I was seeing in myself, because I realized I liked the world a lot better before I knew so much about humans.

This started an identity crisis I would struggle with throughout my career. It was a conflict involving the person I *was* versus the person I was *becoming*. I think of myself as a complicated individual, especially since I tend to analyze things way too much. Trying to figure out who I was supposed to be only made it more confusing. Without a doubt, when I looked at myself in the mirror, I was now seeing two different sides.

CHAPTER 6: TRYOUTS

As we waited for whatever was supposed to happen, nobody said a word. Saying something would seem like nothing more than nervous small talk to ease the tension. Someone started stretching, and the rest of us realized it was a good idea. The occasional glance out the window was hard to resist, because it felt like a storm was on its way. When you looked outside, just across the way, you could see the SERT armory, where they were waiting for us. In just a moment, you'd get to find out what happened to you when you tried out for SERT.

Rumors. We heard them all. We were going to eat so much CS gas that we'd puke. They were going to run us until someone fainted, or puked, or died. We were going to have to hang upside down by our feet from ropes until we could somehow untie ourselves. The rumors varied from Navy SEAL Hell Week stuff to college fraternity pledge material. One thing seemed certain: Most people had a good reason why they would never try out for SERT.

People on the tier or in the office or on the yard can say they were all kinds of things. Sports stars. Amazing shooters. Gazillionth-degree black belts in karate. CrossFit Jedi-masters. Everyone in that room was going to have a chance to show who they were, and the talking part was pretty much over.

At the time, I had about two years in the department. I'd already spent the last year on our Negotiations Management Team (NMT), which was the official name of our hostage negotiations team. I joined the NMT, because I wanted to find more purpose in my job and I was looking for a challenge. Being a correctional officer was not enough for me, because I wasn't getting anything out of it. When I saw a flyer announcing vacancies for the NMT, I submitted an application, wondering if it might make a difference. They picked me up as a negotiator, even though I was still so new in the department.

When I started training in hostage negotiations, I found something I could take pride in. The members of the team were very serious about their training, and they worked very hard on their craft. I jumped into the training with both feet. I began using the skills I learned in every way I could, especially when I was dealing with difficult inmates. I also found ways to use it off duty, for example when negotiating the price of a new car – and even when talking to the occasional disgruntled partner.

Learning about hostage negotiations seemed to couple well with what I studied in psychology. I enjoyed the cerebral aspect of learning how to deescalate a crisis or create win-win situations. I attended all our team trainings and joined the California Association of Hostage Negotiators (CAHN), where we went to seminars and received training and presentations from negotiators who had real-world experience. Training alongside officers from other agencies, many of whom had actually negotiated with hostage takers or suicidal people, made me feel like I was doing something good. Being on the NMT also gave me a chance to see the tactical side of things.

SERT, or the Special Emergency Response Team, was the name of the tactical element of our SWAT program. I noticed the SERT guys whenever we did full-scale exercises, because both teams were present due to their different roles. This is what everyone commonly thinks of SWAT. Same thing, different name. When I saw the SERT team, with all their tac gear and weapons, it reminded me of the Army, which I missed. As much as I enjoyed negotiations, I knew the SERT team was where I really belonged.

The SERT team was a close-knit group, and some people found that to be quite annoying. SERT members always hugged each other. They looked out for each other. They gravitated towards each other when they worked on the yard together. They had Christmas parties and other get-togethers. They also trained very hard, and in the process developed a lot of confidence, which some people may have at times saw as arrogance.

SERT guys had to be in very good shape and had to be outstanding shooters. They spent so much time training with weapons that their weapons handling skills were instantly recognizable out on the range, especially when you saw how smooth their weapons manipulation skills became. What a lot of people didn't get to see was how strong the bond was between the SERT guys, and how it extended all the way across the state. Everyone in the program knew each other, and it was a universal and lifelong bond that started right there on the morning of tryouts. You always remembered the people who were there, because the day became a significant memory marker in your career.

Making it through tryouts changed how you felt about your job from that day forward. It was a career changer, because you found something that mattered to you. Behind every person who tried out, there was a story. Different background. Different experience. Different narrative. Even though not everyone made it to the end of the day, I remember each of their stories very well. It was obvious everyone had different reasons for being there, but the one thing that unified us was that each of us wanted to belong to something we could be proud of. We all wanted our jobs to mean something. As I looked around the room and thought about the different stories in the room, someone finally broke the silence.

"We'd better get out there," someone said. "We're supposed to be in formation by 0630."

"Wait", someone else said. "Did they mean be *here* in formation at 0630, or did they mean be here as in over *there*?"

A conversation than arose in the room about whether or not we should wait right there for them. Having been in the military, my advice was to stay together no matter what we decided to do, because whatever we did, it would be wrong. I was right.

As an act of solidarity, we walked out of the building to go over "there" by the SERT armory. For the first couple of steps, we stood strong and walked together. Then someone started jogging, which urged someone else to start running. Soon everyone was sprinting, because nobody wanted to be last. The next thing we knew we were all standing in the position of attention, and SERT members all came out to take a look at the entertainment. We got yelled at for doing it wrong. *Told you*.

They also yelled at us for a bunch of other stuff that didn't make sense, which reminded me of the military, before taking us over to the two-mile run starting line. That would be the first test. I figured we were going to get some kind of briefing, or maybe some instructions. *Anything*. All I remember is hearing the sound of slapping feet on pavement.

When everyone started running, I was looking down at my watch, trying to push the button to get it over to the stopwatch mode. I scrambled to catch up to all of them, then passed them. I pushed faster and faster, creating more and more space between me and the next person. It was a competition, and the higher score you got, the better chance you had of being selected. At least, that's what was on my mind as I sprinted past them.

I ended up so far out in front that I had no idea where I was supposed to be going. I was still so new at the prison I had never actually been in that area. I came to a Y in the road, and I stopped and jogged in place until everyone caught up. Once they went left, I followed. I caught up to them and passed them again. We eventually arrived at the shooting range, where SERT members in BDUs were waiting, looking very unimpressed.

"12:25!" someone with a timer yelled as I came in.

Like I had just crossed the finish line at the Olympics, I walked around and shook out my limbs. I had been running a lot, and my two-mile run time was averaging around 12 minutes. 12:25 was not too bad, considering the delays, and the way I was walking around made me look like I was quite proud of myself. That was not the right thing to look like, and it gave them something to yell at me for.

"Why did you leave everyone behind?" one of them shouted.

I had to hustle back and find the last man and run in with him. Between having to catch up to the group twice, and then having to go back and run in with the last man, I felt like I had just ran the two-mile run three times. Now, I really was tired, and we hadn't even really started the day yet.

We then climbed some poles, did pushups, sit-ups, pull-ups, and then ran and crawled, and then repeated all the above anytime someone realized it had been too long since we climbed poles, did pushups, sit-ups, ran or crawled. There didn't seem to be an outline or a plan other than trying to see who would quit. Back then, that was the idea. Survive to the end, and be a good partner. Just don't quit.

At one point, I heard someone say "I'm done." I looked over and saw one of the candidates walking off until he crested the hill and disappeared towards the parking lot. If they ever called out to him, I don't remember. I quickly realized that one of us leaving meant more attention for the ones who stayed.

Soon, I saw one of the other candidates turning pale. I figured he was done as he bent over, opened his mouth wide, and vomited right there by his feet. He wiped his face with the back of his hand, shrugged and went on. They started yelling at us again for more stuff, and we were off to the next test.

We ran up hills and then down hills, and then all around different parts of the prison property that covered acres and acres of terrain. We occasionally stopped to do more pushups, burpees and sit-ups, just to wear us out and to see if anyone would quit. We ended up all the way at the edge of the prison property, down the long perimeter dirt road. When we rounded the corner by the fence line, we stopped as we saw the next test in front of us.

I don't know if I've ever seen water so black and so gooey. The stench was prominent, even back where we were standing. This particular part of the prison property was where a local rancher allowed his cattle to freely roam. Cow patties littered the entire hillside like land mines, and the occasional decomposed remains of a dead cow made it seem almost like a cattle cemetery.

As I stared at the dark water, I felt myself gag. For a second, I thought I saw some kind of dark, floaty thing surface and then sink back down again. No, I thought to myself, this is about to get wrong. Before you could say *gastrointestinal distress*, they started screaming at us to get into the water. We frantically splashed into the water as if we were triathletes at the sound of the starting gun. I tried to keep my mouth above the water to no avail. The pushups were bearable, because the water had a way of lifting you up. The sit-ups sucked, because the water found its way into your nostrils as you laid back. Then, if you gasped for air, the foul water found its way into your mouth as well.

In a weird, gross kind of way, the water was refreshing, because it was a hot summer day. But it only felt good on the *outside* of your body. Inside your mouth, not so good. They made us do exercises long enough to be amused, and then yelled at us to get out of the water hole. This particular part of the tryout day ended up being quite memorable, because it not only cooled us off, but lifted our spirits in a silly, frolic kind of way. We would end up making sure we always kept it in the agenda as a tryout tradition, and we affectionately called them "bubble-ups."

Covered in mud, we were herded over to a rescue litter sitting on the ground filled with weights. They didn't even think to make it look like we were rescuing something human. We were just rescuing heavy shit. Dumbbells. Rocks. Junk. Our bodies wobbled as we lifted the litter and began carrying it all over the hillside. No particular destination seemed to be waiting for us. It took everything we had to keep the momentum moving forward. They were continuously yelling at us to go faster, and the hoarseness in their voices showed us the day had been long for them as well.

We tried to pump our legs faster, but the best we could do was drag each foot forward, one at a time, until it passed the other foot just enough to create some forward movement. Still covered in mud, we looked like zombies. The muck covering every inch of our bodies began to dry to a crispy, cake-like consistency, making it even harder to move. I felt relief whenever they stopped us for pushups, because it was nice to set that heavy rescue litter down. Every time we did so, I had to physically peel my cramped, curled fingers off the metal bar to let go.

After slushing around the hillside for what seemed like an eternity, we were finally told to put the litter down. There wasn't a finish line, a checkered flag, or even an observable endpoint. They simply had seen enough of us running around grunting and groaning like cattle. They had us leave the litter on the ground so we could run up a long, steep hill back towards the shooting range. Even without the rescue litter, the cramping in our thighs caused our feet to continuously drag in the dirt, causing more and more dust to cake all over us. It felt impossible to run.

Two of the candidates were struggling and falling back. The regular SERT members smelled blood and swarmed in to see if they could finish them off and get them to quit. We tried to motivate our fading partners by yelling at them to keep going, but when you are that tired, just mustering up the energy to vocalize sucks away what little energy you have left. We even tried to physically push them up the hill, but one of the candidates couldn't go any further. Once he stopped and told them he quit, they took him away. Little did he realize the top of that hill was the end of the run.

It felt good to finally stop, but we knew it was not going to be a rest, considering the telephone pole under the team commander's boot. As usual, he was standing there looking at us unimpressed. It was pretty obvious what we were supposed to do next – pick the stupid pole up. So that's what we did. We bent over in unison and grunted as we all lifted it to our shoulders. It was a lot heavier than it looked. Then, they had us put it back down. Ahhh. Then, we had to pick it back up. Ummph. Then back down. Back up. Back down. Up. Down. Up. Down. Ahhh. Ummph. Ahhh. Ummph.

Then we did sit-ups with the pole across our chests. Then we stood up with it and did shoulder presses. Lifting it overhead was excruciating for me, because sometime during the rescue litter carry I pulled something in my back. I couldn't stand upright, much less lift my arms up high. I kept hoping for more pushups just so I didn't have to stand. Quitting was not an option, but I was definitely having a hard time dealing with the pain. It seemed to get worse by the minute.

At one point, I happened to look up to the sky as we were doing sit-ups. The clouds, cotton-like, were silently crawling from left to right, and the bluest sky peaked through the leaves through surrounding oak trees.

Are you seriously feeling sorry for yourself? Does your wittle backy hurt? Hmm? Are you so beat down and self-absorbed you can't even look around you and notice the trees, and the clouds, and the blue sky up there? Really?

That thought flipped a switch in me. My thoughts went back to the Army, as I remembered what it felt like to fight for something. There was no way I was about to go back to being the type of person who let someone get in my head. I told myself there isn't a fucking thing these guys can dish out that will ever make me quit - I didn't care how much longer we had to go through with this. Plus, when you know the guy to your right isn't going to quit, and the guy to your left isn't going to quit, it is a feeling like nothing else in the world, and you know you owe it to them to keep going. That was the first moment in my career when I actually felt like I was where I was supposed to be.

CHAPTER 7: PTM

A Potential Team Member, or PTM, was someone who made it through tryouts and was selected to be on the team. Your job as a PTM was to prepare for the SERT academy, which only came around once a year. That meant if you weren't ready to go to the academy, or if you went but couldn't graduate, you'd have to wait a full year before your next chance.

We trained relentlessly. If we weren't at the range working on tactical shooting, we were learning room entry and hostage rescue techniques. On our team, they also made sure there was plenty of running and crawling around scheduled. The theory back then was the more discomfort you felt during training, the less discomfort you would feel going through the SERT academy. To help us out with that, they made sure our training time was as uncomfortable as possible. They were looking out for us, I guess.

At the time, the H&K stance was the shooting stance we learned, which must have been invented by some sadistic person who had no feeling in his lower back. Being out on the range for several hours in the hot sun shooting shotguns, handguns or carbines always made me wonder what kind of irreparable damage I was doing to my spine as I held myself in that stance.

"If it hurts, then you're doing it right!" That's what we'd hear from behind us, and I'd always think how much easier it was to say that when you weren't the one bent over in that stance. Before hearing this motto, I was of the mind that if something hurt, then it was most likely trying tell you to *stop doing that,* because something ain't right. As PTMs, we developed really strong backs.

Learning entry techniques was painful too. It was pretty much understood if you were clearing rooms and realized the shooter was in the next room, you'd better get in there and get him no matter how many simunition rounds were flying at you, striking your fingers, groin and sensitive thigh areas.

We'd cringe as we heard the words "Down to your T-shirts!" That meant we kept our face, neck and groin protection on, but we'd be down to our T-shirts, just to make sure we knew when we were hit. We each had simunition scars on our bodies that would never, ever go away. Those little simunition rounds had a mischievous mind of their own and always found the most sensitive areas of our bodies.

There was a lot of reinforcement utilized in this learning process, and damn if that wasn't one more thing that reminded me of my psychology classes. During room entries, any hesitation or sign of indecisiveness was reprimanded with the use of a simunition round delivered into your butt cheek, just to make you not want to make the same mistake again. Positive punishment. Psychology 101.

"Everyone set up again outside, except you," the instructor would sometimes say to someone.

"Me?"

"Yes, you."

"But I was…"

"Wrong. Why were you looking over to the right?"

"Because I, well, I was... Well, I fucked up, sir. That's why."

"That's right. *You fucked up.* And because you weren't covering your AOR, your partner got shot in the back. Turn around."

From the other room, we could hear the familiar crack of a simunition round accompanied by the "Umph" of a PTM grunting.

The punishment wasn't always away-from-view execution style. Sometimes we'd get shot right in the ass as we were moving through the site. We'd be clearing rooms and hear "Crack!" Then we noticed that one of our partners suddenly grabbed his butt cheek and stood up straight, cursing under his breath. Someone's partner failed to block and cover for them. *That's right, you fucked up.* Sometimes, the whole stick got shot in the ass because none of us checked down the hallway. To us, that seemed kind of weird, since we *just came from down that hallway and all.* Arguing your point or being right was not going to change things, and if you argued too much, "Crack!"

One day, we decided enough was enough. While stacked up outside the doorway waiting for the next entry, we decided no matter what the scenario was, we would charge in and light the instructor up with a barrage of simunition rounds. And that was exactly what we did. Nobody got shot in the ass again after that.

It was an aggressive style of training, so we became an aggressive group of people. It got to the point where we were all trying to squeeze in front of each other as we stacked up at the breach point, just so we could be the first one in. You wanted to be the guy who found the fight. You wanted the tango to be in your side of the room. If he wasn't, you were disappointed.

After countless force-on-force repetitions, our OODA cycle (Observe, Orent, Decide and Act) became extremely smooth and extremely fast. There weren't many variables we hadn't seen, because there are only so many combinations of corners and closets and doorways that you can place suspects, hostages and unknowns in. Once you realize that the suspect's behavior determines your actions, the mental processes you run through became smoother and smoother with each repetition. Especially after several years of this type of training and literally hundreds, if not thousands of repetitions it got to the point where the more experienced guys didn't even get their heart rate up anymore as they moved from room to room.

It is a type of training that brings you and your partners very close, because you develop a lot of trust in each other. You also see how hard everyone is working, which invokes a lot of mutual respect for each other. It reminded me of being in the Army because of how close the friendships were. The type of friendships you have in the military are different from the friendships you have as a civilian, just like the friendships you have on the SERT team are different from the friendships you have outside of SERT. It doesn't necessarily make those relationships better or worse, or more or less significant, but there is simply a different level of trust among people you've worked so hard with, especially those who you fought alongside to get through something physically and mentally challenging with. You feel like there is a type of relationship there that you don't really have with other people. It's one thing to have friends, but it is a different thing to have friends who you know will never give up on you no matter how hot, cold, wet or tired they are. After leaving the military, I had no reason to think I'd experience that kind of thing again.

I had a lot of friends who weren't on the SERT team. They were guys I fished with, hunted with, went to see major league baseball games with, played fantasy football with, and guys I hung out and drank beer with. I even got together to play music with a few of them. I never really thought that I would get disconnected from the non-SERT aspects of our department, because I saw myself as more than just a *SERT Guy*.

Eventually, it started to happen though. The longer you were in the SERT program, the more you realized you were at odds with the way routine processes were dealt with during your regular job. During SERT trainings or emergency activations, the work involved was different from what it was like on your job as a regular correctional officer. In your regular job, you noticed a lot of people getting favors because they knew somebody. Not on the SERT team, though. Everything you got on SERT, including your reputation, was based on your work ethic and your performance. It didn't matter who you drank with.

The SERT program was also exempt from whatever it is in our department that extinguishes ambition in people. Our department really didn't support the idea of its employees thinking too much for themselves, and this created a lot of micromanagement. As a PTM in the SERT program, you experienced leadership rather than management, because the primary goal of the instructors and the leaders in the SERT program was to push you to constantly grow and get better. I can't say our department, at least when it came to the day-to-day management of people, ever really made people feel that way. Some managers even made it fairly obvious that what they were most interested in was the next promotion. Or at least that is the perception many of us had.

If I sound a little bitter, it is because I didn't like the way some supervisors and managers went about their jobs. Maybe if it wasn't for the SERT team, I wouldn't have thought a difference in leadership was even possible in our department. There was a lot of silliness going on, like state-wide decisions that sometimes made no sense, but you had to follow each directive. After all, someone somewhere thought it made sense and they put it in writing in some policy. Do it, or be punished. That is how the department worked. On the contrary, in SERT, everything made sense.

There was a sigh of relief when you looked at the calendar and saw you had SERT training coming up. SERT membership was something we earned. It wasn't given to you just because you put in a letter of interest or you interviewed. You didn't get to be on the SERT team because someone liked you. Nobody shot your target for you or wore all that gear for you. Nobody ran for you or crawled through the obstacle course for you. Nobody went through the force-on-force threat level assessments for you or decided what level of force was required for you. All those things you had to do yourself, and if you didn't do it right, you didn't meet the standards. If you didn't meet the standards, it was pretty clear: you didn't really want it badly enough, and you had to accept that the program was not for you. There were no hard feelings about that. We loved the SERT team because nobody was exempt from the standards.

Being a PTM was rewarding because you were constantly getting better, whether it was your shot groups or your smooth movement through a crisis site. The thing you quickly noticed when you joined the team was that the best SERT members where the type who were never satisfied with their level of skills.

Every team has those guys who excel beyond the others. They are the type that no matter what standard you place in front of them, they will not stop just because they have reached it. As you get to know them, you realize it is really quite simple: they find every opportunity to seek improvement. They never sit back, comfortable with where they are. Some people call it a "warrior mindset," because they constantly fight and battle to improve every chance they have. As a PTM, you quickly identified who those people were, and if you were smart, you emulated them. In a sense, they made you realize if you truly want to excel at something, you should never stop acting like a PTM, who is constantly fighting to improve.

CHAPTER 8: GUITAR SOLO

The FM radio in the yard office had speaker wire taped to the antennae. The wire then ran up along the walls and draped over the pipes at the ceiling like a big spider web. It was our makeshift radio antennae – a little trick we learned from the inmates. It was interesting to see how something we might usually take for granted, like a local radio station, can provide a sense of normalcy within such an abnormal place, where the thick walls blocked radio signals coming from the outside world. I'm sure it was the primary reason why inmates listened to music on their headphones all the time, and it was why the radio played in our office continuously. It had a way of getting your mind off being in prison.

A song finished on the radio, and we paused to listen to an announcement as we got ready to head out onto the tier to count the inmates. The radio station, Rock 104, was having a guitar solo contest. Anyone who wanted to enter the contest was supposed to call in and play a guitar solo over the phone. The winner of the contest would play *Take Me Out to the Ballgame* standing on top of the dugout for opening day at our local minor league ballpark, John Thurman Field. As the field had undergone millions of dollars in upgrades in the offseason, the opening day celebration was supposed to be a major event with thousands of people expected to be present.

"Hey," one of my partners said. "Don't you play the guitar? You should enter that contest."

I thought about how many guitarists would be calling in, and I said with a laugh, "Like some prison guard would ever win that guitar solo contest."

"Oh, okay. I guess you're *scared*."

Working in prison isn't much different from being back in elementary school. Not only do people make fun of you a lot, but they also call you names and pick on you, especially if they like you. And being called "scared" still does the same thing to you as it did back in elementary school.

As we walked through the housing unit to count the inmates, I couldn't get my mind off that contest. Should I? *Nah.* Maybe that ship has sailed. I was also worried that if I entered some guitar solo contest and embarrassed myself, it would only make it much more real that I had become a prison guard, rather than a musician. I wondered if my fingers could even move like they once did on the fretboard. I hadn't played much guitar, because I was spending every bit of my spare time training for SERT. But scared? No way. Your MOM is scared, that's what!

It turns out I had something to prove, and not only because grown-ups still hate being called scared. I just couldn't let a guitar solo contest on my favorite radio station pass by without entering. I had to enter it.

The next day, I called the radio station. The popular local DJ, who went by the name Sausage, immediately answered the phone, catching me off guard. I asked him if the contest was still going on, and he told me it was the last day.

"If you have a solo, let's hear it," he said in his radio DJ voice.

With the phone against my ear, I ran upstairs and started grabbing guitar cords.

"Uh, one second. Here's one. No, wait not that one. I'm sorry, Sausage, I'm trying to find a cord."

As I was plugging into my amp, I asked him how many people had entered the contest. "I've been listening to guitar solos all week."

I'm wasting my time, I thought.

Finally, I turned on the amplifier and set the phone down on the carpet in front of it.

"Okay, here we go." With that, I started playing my own interpretation of *Take Me Out to the Ballgame*.

At the end, I held the last open chord long enough to let it feedback through my amp a few seconds before picking the phone up off the ground. I figured, *Yep, I blew it*. As I brought the phone up to my ear, I was actually going to apologize, when I heard him yelling on his side of the phone.

"Yeeeaaah!!! That was AWESOME! I'll call you tomorrow to let you know if you won."

He had to be telling everyone that, because there was no way I would be getting that call.

The next day, I was watching TV when my phone rang.

"Rob?"

"Yeah?"

"Hey, this is Sausage from Rock 104. What are you doing tomorrow?"

"Uhhhh…."

"Well, good! Because tomorrow you need to be standing on top of the dugout playing guitar at opening day."

"You're kidding me."

"No, I'm not. Head down to the radio station today and pick up your tickets. They'll give you all the details."

"Wait a second," I said shaking my head to clear it. "You're telling me I *won*?"

"Of course you won!" he said.

"How many other people won?" I asked.

"Dude, one. *You*."

I hung up and jumped in the car and drove right down to the radio station before they could change their mind. As I checked in with the receptionist, I told her I was there to get tickets to opening day. She told me the game was completely sold out and they already gave away all their tickets. I told her Sausage said I was supposed to get tickets for the guitar solo thing, and as soon as I said it, she cried out.

"Oh! You won the *guitar contest*!" She turned around and yelled down the hallway. "Hey, the guitar solo winner is here!"

Two employees walked out from the back to meet me. They seemed a lot more excited about the whole thing than I was, making me wonder how big this event was really supposed to be. They handed me my free tickets and told me where I was supposed to meet the event coordinator at the ball park. Before I walked out, the receptionist turned to me again.

"I hope you don't have trouble playing in front of people." Seeing the confused look on my face, she added, "They're expecting five thousand people at the ballpark."

I almost handed the tickets right back to her.

On opening day, I showed up at the ball park with my guitar case and amplifier in my hands, not too much unlike how I showed up at Schofield Barracks. I located the administrative office, and as I walked in, I could tell the lady behind the counter was someone important. She was frazzled and was walking back and forth, giving directions to people. Whether it was to people in the office or on the phone, which was still up to her ear, I wasn't sure.

I waited patiently as she talked to someone on the other end about skydivers and how much wind would cause them to have to cancel their jump into the park. *Wow, skydivers. This is cool.*

"Oh, good!" She looked down at my guitar and amplifier. "The guitar guy, right?"

"Right."

"Okay, take your stuff down to the top of the home team dugout. There is an electrical outlet there. Plug it in and leave everything sitting on the side of the dugout in a little spot right there. Go back down there in the middle of the seventh. We'll put your amp on top of the dugout. As soon as I tell you to, play your song and quickly get off the dugout. No delay. We have a really tight timeline, because a lot of stuff is happening in each inning. Understand?"

I had some questions. A lot, actually. Like will there be a microphone the amp will play into, should I leave the guitar there when I'm done or should I carry everything back, or… She didn't give me a chance to ask any questions; she went right back to her phone.

"No, the potato sack race is in the fifth inning, not the *second!*"

I walked down to the home field dugout and set my guitar and amplifier down near it. I wondered if I was supposed to do a sound check, but the stands were quickly filling with fans, and I figured it wouldn't be cool to attract everyone's attention by plugging in to see how it sounded. I could just imagine that lady running down towards me, yelling like First Sergeant Stanley.

I went to find my seat, which was right behind home plate. The person sitting in the next seat introduced himself as Sausage from Rock 104. *No way!* He didn't even look like whatever a radio DJ is supposed to look like – he was a regular, clean-cut dude. He handed me a Rock 104 T-shirt and told me the radio station wanted me to wear it during the solo.

It was cool to sit next to him. This was before satellite radio had become popular, so everyone listened to the local radio stations. He was sort of a celebrity in our area because if you liked rock music, you listened to Rock 104. I had heard his voice on the radio so many times I couldn't believe I was actually sitting next to him chatting it up as if we were old friends. The stands filled, and even the concrete perimeter walkways were packed with people who had standing room only tickets.

Just as they had been advertising over the radio, the event was very lively. As we watched the game, Sausage and I talked about rock music and our favorite guitar players, and it was pretty cool that we had the same taste in both.

Before I knew it, it was the middle of the seventh and I had to make my way down to the dugout. The spunky event lady was there waiting for me with a microphone in her hand. They already had my amplifier up on top of the dugout, and as I walked up, some staffer guy in a yellow jacket slipped my guitar over my shoulder. I felt like a rock star going out on stage. The event lady pointed to her watch and leaned over into my face.

"You have two minutes and 30 seconds. Starting... Now! Get up there, *you're on!*"

It felt as if a million butterflies were scattering around inside my stomach. As I jumped up onto the dugout, I got to see a different perspective of what 5,000 people looked like. She introduced me as the *Rock 104 Guitar Solo Contest Winner*, and for a brief moment, the crowd fell silent.

"Rrrrrrrob Sharrrrrrkeyyyyy!"

Holy shit, this is happening. I glanced down at the amplifier and noticed the power light wasn't on. I could actually hear the crowd murmur a little as if some realized something wasn't right. I was thinking "*Oh, please do not tell me they forgot to plug it into the outlet.*" I reached down, flicked down on the power button, and the amplifier popped to life, which is always an awesome sound, no matter if you are in your back room at home or on a dugout at a baseball stadium. As I started playing, the players down in the dugout all came out to watch me play.

At the end of the song, I let the last three notes of the song ring out for the "oooold baaaaall gaaaaaaame" part, and the crowd sang the words along with my guitar. I held onto the last chord and let it feedback for a moment, because I figured I would probably never get this chance again. I had waited a long time to know what this felt like. I pointed at my Rock 104 shirt as the crowd cheered, and then handed the guitar back to the guy in the yellow jacket before jumping down off the dugout.

The crowd's cheering quickly quieted as the pitcher went into his windup for the first pitch of the inning. And just like that, it was over. I made my way back to my seat, and some guy high-fived me as I walked by. I don't remember a single moment of the rest of that game.

They, whoever they are, say the person you are at work should be the person you are all the time. *Don't change who you are* – that's what they tell you when you get a job as a correctional officer. *Don't try to become someone you're not.* There is nothing worse than people who are trying too hard to be something they aren't. The question is: Who are you?

If I were to take a really good look at myself in the mirror, and then attempt to answer the question, "Who am I?" the answer would depend on what time of day it was.

After winning that contest and playing the guitar on top of the dugout, I started making more time to play the guitar. I realized it had a way of reminding me of not only who I was, but maybe more importantly, of something I needed in my life. At work, I became known as a *SERT Guy*. When you're a SERT Guy, it sort of defines not just what kind of officer you are supposed to be, but also what kind of *person* you are supposed to be. SERT guys are supposed to be squared away. They should be the first ones into the fight if there was trouble. They were the guys who fought for and believed in a cause. They were so motivated and driven that it was annoying to other people.

The SERT guys were hard chargers, always pushing themselves and others to be better at what they did. That means people expected you to carry yourself at a higher standard, and if you didn't, you weren't who you said you were. While being a correctional officer was a job, joining the SERT team was something that effected your life. You couldn't just dabble in it.

The guitar solo contest made me realize playing the guitar was important to me, because it reminded me of a side of my personality that would always need to exist, no matter what kind of job I had. Maybe in a sense, it was even more important to keep it up now, considering I was also doing the SWAT thing. Playing the guitar kept me balanced; I needed to remember that I was much more than a prison guard, or a SWAT guy. It made me realize it feels good to find time to do what you love. This is what defines you, and if you don't use it, you may lose it.

CHAPTER 9: SERT ACADEMY

After checking our IDs, the Army E-4 Specialist at the guard shack asked us to pull aside and step out of the van. This was obviously not the normal protocol. We nervously exited our van, wondering what we did wrong. As we stood off to the side, I noticed a fenced area where some old helicopters and small military aircraft were stored. I realized this was the first time I had been on a military base since getting out of the Army. Camp San Luis Obispo was not like the military bases I was used to. It was more like a pseudo, reduced version of the real thing. It was unassuming and peaceful, and there weren't as many troops marching and running around. I wondered if we were at the right place, until I saw the "37th Basic SERT Academy" sign posted at the front gate.

Before we took off from home, the older guys on our team told us stories about their SERT academies. They told us about how they showed up on base and the cadre instructors were all over them, screaming and trying to trip them up right out of the gate. To get through the course and graduate, you simply had to survive all the way to the end, while avoiding an injury that might get you sent home. Guys would hide their injuries from detection, even serious ones at times, just because they wanted to graduate so badly. Back then, the number one goal of the SERT academy was to see if you could make it to the end. Those who graduated with a certificate had something to be proud of.

I was pretty sure I could take the yelling and the theatrics. Physically, I felt ready too. I was doing everything I could think of to prepare for the course. Aside from my regular workouts, I was doing a ton of pushups, pull-ups and sit-ups to prepare for whatever they were going to dish out. I also started to follow training programs for marathon runners and triathletes, just to make sure I was doing everything I could to prepare, alternating long runs with high intensity intervals. I'd go over to the local high school and jump the fence to the track, just to make sure I was running the intervals exactly as scheduled.

If even half of the stories were true about the SERT academy, we were about to get swarmed by deranged cadre. I figured it would be the typical welcome you got to most paramilitary style courses, and nothing I hadn't had to deal with before. I reminded myself to play along with the game and not to draw attention to myself. I heard so many different stories, like one guy getting so stressed out during in-processing that he dropped his carbine rifle onto the pavement out in the parking lot. The crunch of a carbine crashing into concrete is fairly unmistakable, and every cadre within hearing distance ran over to scream at him. *Don't be that guy,* I told myself, as I looked around for incoming cadre.

"Hey, someone's coming," one of my partners said.

I looked down the road and saw someone on a mountain bike heading in our direction. As he got closer, I realized it was a lieutenant from our SERT team at our prison who they brought down to run the SERT academy that year. He had been in SERT for a long time, and he came up through the SERT team at Deuel Vocational Center (DVI), a prison that prides itself in being called the "gladiator school" of the prison system.

When Ty first transferred to our prison, it didn't take long to see a uniqueness about him that separated him from others just by the way he carried himself. He always looked sharp and stayed in incredible shape, and even years later when he reached the age of retirement, he looked like he could knock out a hundred pushups like it was nothing.

He had a bright, toothy smile and a long, snow white handlebar mustache that flirted with departmental grooming standards. It gave him the look of being someone you didn't want to mess with, even though if you were lucky enough to know him, you would consider him one of the nicest men you ever met. That said, he was definitely old school.

As he got closer to us on his bike, I wondered how many pushups we were going to have to do. I took a deep breath. *Okay, here we go.*

"What's up, guys?" He jumped off his bike with a big smile.

We snapped to parade rest. It just seemed like the right thing do to. He didn't have time for any of that, nor did he feel like having us run around and do pushups or assume the dying cockroach position. He didn't yell at us or ask us what our major malfunction was either. He didn't even call us maggots. He simply wanted to check on his guys to make sure they made the drive safely. He snapped our photo in front of the *37th Basic SERT Academy* sign and rode off. It was definitely not the reception we were expecting.

That night, I couldn't sleep. I lay awake staring at the ceiling, listening to everyone in the barracks snore away in their bunks. As the night dragged on, every hour was marked by a symphony of hourly chimes as wristwatches throughout the bay signaled that another hour had gone by. After a couple of hours of this, it started driving me nuts. I tried to relax, but my mind raced with pent-up energy. This, for me, had become more than just some SWAT course. It was more than that. It was my way of finding something that mattered. It was a chance to do something I could be proud of. Let's face it, there are plenty of television shows, books and movies that honor the service of distinguished people like police officers, firemen, and specialized units within the armed forces, but, nobody out there ever thinks being a correctional officer is very impressive. When children talk about what they are going to be when they grow up, no kid ever says he wants to become a prison guard. This was our way of making our job cool. As I twisted and turned, trying to get my mind to stop racing, I was wishing they had thrashed us when we showed up earlier that morning. It would have at least made it easier to sleep. Now, I was going to begin the SERT academy on the first day already sleep deprived.

Before I knew it, everyone was up, fixing their bunks and getting ready for the course to start. I looked around and noticed how rested everyone looked but me. I looked down at my bunk and suddenly realized if they just allowed me to crawl back into my bunk, I might be able to fall asleep in seconds. Doug, one of my best friends from our team back home, was in the bunk next to me. He peeked his head around his locker and with a big smile he said, "Welcome to Day Zero!"

Day Zero was qualifications day. That meant a full day of running around, and it wasn't even going to count as an official day of training yet. We'd have to run the two-mile run, go through the obstacle course, and then shoot weapons qualifications just to get accepted into the SERT academy. If you passed everything, you could stay. If you didn't, you went home. It was that simple.

Day Zero ended up being different from the stories we had heard. The instructors and cadre treated us like professionals, and it was all quite a contrast to what went on at earlier academies. Maybe they figured it was probably a good idea not to try to stress out people who were running around with guns.

Camp San Luis Obispo had just enough necessary facilities to hold a SERT academy. It had barracks, a dining hall, shooting ranges and even a MOUT (Military Operations on Urban Terrain) site. The MOUT site, situated at the end of one of the range roads, had a large multi-story building for entry operations training. Although it was built to withstand flash bangs and other abuses of military and law enforcement use, the interior doors always ended up hanging cockeyed in the door frame by the time the course was over. We weren't supposed to kick the doors, but the foot-shaped holes approximately three feet off the ground were evidence it was difficult to temper the excitement when you're doing hostage rescue training.

The base was fairly lackluster as far as military bases go, but it was interesting to see some of the old deteriorated military buildings still standing – they provided an antique snapshot of its history going back before World War I, when it was once called Camp Merriam. Although most of the buildings on the base were abandoned, several newer buildings were erected to prove that the base was still in use. Along the range road that went out the training sites, a few remains of the artillery camp and its mess hall still existed, but they were a faded imprint of what they once used to be.

In the main part of the base, many of the small "hooches" still remained at that time, which were three-man huts many of us heard about from earlier SERT academies. Back when earlier SERT academy participants had to sleep in them, they provided very little comfort and protection from the elements. They often had to sleep with a poncho draped over their heads when it rained. The newer barracks were much better, even though we would spend very little time in them.

Overall, the 37th Basic SERT academy started with 62 participants. Most of us were correctional officers from the California Department of Corrections prisons scattered throughout the state of California. It was common to have a few non-CDC personnel go through the SERT academy – some of them were military Special Forces, other state correctional systems, other law enforcement agencies, or even military/special forces guys from other countries. Our academy had a couple of officers from the Utah Department of Corrections SWAT program, someone from Finland, and two SWAT officers from Brazil.

The two Brazilians were attached to my squad. One look at either of those two characters, and you probably wouldn't assume they were SWAT guys. They were small, silly, and usually smiling ear to ear, at least during the first few days of the course. With each passing day, we saw less and less of their beaming smiles, as they started looking at us like we were from a different planet. You could tell they began to wonder what the hell was wrong with all these loco American guys, never resting and going all day like this.

Finally, it became quite apparent it was all too much for them, because they started dialing it down big time. To them, no matter what happened at our SERT academy in the U.S., they would still go home to Brazil and be SWAT guys. To us, things were not that way. We cherished every second of the course, because we knew we had only one shot at it. If you didn't graduate and were lucky enough to be kept on your team at home, it would be as a PTM for another year. Screw that.

Some of the guys were sent home that first day (Day 0) because they failed to pass the entrance quals. Others were sent home due to injuries. One of the guys fell and broke his wrist while doing "spider drops" out at the range. Spider drops are these Spiderman-like maneuvers that allow you to drop off the edge of a small building by dangling off the edge. He ended up breaking his wrist and had to be sent home. He looked devastated when he showed up at the chow hall to say goodbye to us, with his wrist in a cast. I felt really bad for him, and I could only silently shake my head. I hated spider drops.

At the halfway point of the course, everyone was looking pretty tore up. Everyone was in very good shape physically, but the lack of sleep and constant movement from one training to the next started to wear on us. We conducted every conceivable variation of hostage rescue they could think of, and as much fun as it was, it became obvious how tired we were anytime we stopped for the next class. As the next lecture was given to us, our heads would nod uncontrollably. You tried to listen, but you would sometimes catch yourself zoning out for a moment until you realized it was time to stack up on the door for the next entry. We assaulted buses, cars, stairwells, buildings, hallways, open places, small places and everything in between. Believe me, that first night was the only night I had trouble falling asleep.

Our two drill instructors were hard on us, just like they were supposed to be. I was scolded anytime I said "Hooah" because it is an Army thing. In the Army, "Hooah" means yes, okay, sure, I got it, 10-4, and it can also mean "squared away" as in *that dude is totally Hooah*. It means anything you want it to mean. Even though the DIs didn't like Army things, I felt obligated to continue saying "Hooah." Having been in the infantry, it was just one of those things that came out of my mouth without much thought. I said it so much that after we graduated, Doug bought me a T-shirt that said "HOOAH" on it.

Although I couldn't bring myself to say "Ew-rah," I did accept the fact that most SERT things seemed to come from the Marine Corps. The way we conducted weapon zeroing, the acronyms we memorized, our operations orders format, and even our BDU hats were from the Marine Corps. Our DI's even called cadence with a "Left, right, ah-layo, left, righty, lay-yo…" When the DIs found out I could call cadence and lead formations, I got to step out and call the cadence for our runs. As much as I enjoyed the USMC style of cadence, I had to stay true to my roots. *Hooah*.

Just like at the academy, I came up with cadence calls for us, making them about SERT rather than about jumping out of an airplane into a combat zone. Singing cadence was a lot like performing a song: You dug down deep and gave it everything you had, from your soul. There is something about the sound of everyone echoing back, like a concerto, that I could never get tired of. It makes you feel like you can run all day. As far as I was concerned, our runs during the SERT academy were never long enough.

I was proud to have attended (and graduated) the 37th Basic SERT Academy, because the last basic SERT Academy would be the 40th Academy, in 2002. After that, the SERT program became the CRT (Crisis Response Team) program, and the tactical (SERT) and negotiator (NMT) elements were combined onto one team. The certification courses for negotiator and tactical members remained separate courses. I am proud that I was able to experience what it was like before and after the change, because it taught me something very important about forward momentum.

What we knew as the "SERT Academy" became a thing of the past, as the certification process for the tactical operators became two separate courses: the CRT Level I Operator (OP I) and CRT Level II Operator (OP II) course. This two-tiered certification process basically took the old SERT academy and doubled it, since two separate certification courses would now have to be completed.

You have to continue to move forward and evolve if you want to remain relevant. This applies to everything, no matter if you are in a SWAT program, a small business, a sports program, or even in a bar band. There were a lot of older, experienced SERT members who resisted change, and if they had had their way and the program hadn't changed, the program could have lost its relevance years ago. The old SERT academies went away because as SWAT tactics and equipment evolved, there was far too much material to cover in just one course.

In those early days of SERT, if you had heart, you could make the team. If you didn't, you wouldn't. Looking back, I sometimes miss those days, because there wasn't as much fancy gear, expensive gadgets or big words. We had to make the best with what we had, and you were tested by being thrown into the fight to see if you had any heart. The main thing they wanted to know was that you would never quit on your partners.

The problem with not evolving and sticking with older methods was that people got broken. They pushed themselves harder and harder to show they wouldn't quit, and then something in their bodies had to give way – a leg, a hamstring, a shoulder. Our entire squad at our SERT academy was limping around and nursing injuries. Our squad bay always smelled like a BENGAY factory.

Now, the CRT program is much better, because the formula is better. If you want to stay relevant, you have to get smarter. You have to get mission-specific. You have to maintain a goal of effective, intelligent training, and that means effective repetitions of what you are going to have to do to live, and you do this by starting slow and then working up to speed. This is exactly what it takes to be a good guitar player too, because when people try to move too fast or jump too far forward, it is only a matter of time before their guitars end up sitting in their closet. They lose interest, because they've been playing all this time and still can't groove. There is something ridiculously simple and effective about practicing the basics over and over again. I learned this as a guitar player, but I had it verified when I saw our CRT program evolve.

If only they could just find a better way to do spider drops! By the time you read this, maybe they have.

CHAPTER 10: FEEDING THE DOG

An old hunter and his two dogs were longtime buddies and competitive hunting partners. As soon as the old man grabbed his shotgun, those two dogs would be pacing back and forth at the front door, wagging their tails, flapping their tongues, unable to contain their excitement. There was nothing in the world they loved more than retrieving birds. The thing about retrieving a bird, though, is that it's a one-dog operation. There can't be a tie. One dog per bird. The ongoing competition between the two made them better hunting dogs because they pushed each other. You either got faster and smarter, or you fell behind.

Our instructor gathered us around for a little pep talk and told us about the hunting dog story. He was the kind of instructor who had a very charismatic way about him, and he had a knack for making you push to get better. He was tall and lanky, without an ounce of fat on his body, and his confidence and mannerisms evidenced many years of training. He was the kind of guy who would give you the shirt off his back, but who'd also put a boot in your ass. His penchant for coming up with unconventional training methods usually pushed the limits, which often had those in charge silently say their prayers as they watched from a distance. We loved training with him because he made you believe in what you were doing. After all, that was an important aspect of what we were trying to do, because we wanted this to matter. His way of pushing you put a fire into you, and at the end of every training you knew you put in work that day.

On the day he told us that hunting dog story, we were conducting weapon retention and defensive tactics techniques. That kind of training was never a day without bumps and bruises, and he was using the story to keep us in the fight.

"Who can tell me which of the two dogs won?" he asked after telling us the story.

After a long silence, it was obvious nobody had an answer, so he said, "It was the dog the hunter *fed better*."

He scanned us with his eyes, the same way a head coach would look over his team during halftime. It was supposed to be an *Aha* moment, so I nodded my head up and down like I totally got it, but I had no clue what he was talking about. The dog who ate better was the one who got the bird? Whaaat?

I wondered how this had anything at all to do with SWAT training. Maybe it was a lesson about nutrition. Eat better and you will perform better. I mouthed the words to myself. *The dog that won… was the dog the hunter fed better.* Maybe it meant the old man fed the dog that brought back the bird as a reward. So if you win, you get to eat. It pays to be a winner.

The training went on. A handgun was made safe, checked, and then double-checked by showing the empty chamber to everyone. Once we all verified the weapon was empty, we were brought forward, two at a time, to sit on the ground facing away from each other. The empty gun was placed on the ground between the two. This was a few years before training guns like Blueguns were used for this kind of thing, so there was a bit of a pucker factor involved. Even though the gun was checked by everyone, your mind still believed there could be a round in that chamber.

When we heard "Threat!" we were supposed to turn and fight our opponent for the gun. In the process, shirts got ripped, bodies got nicked, and egos got bruised. Since I had wrestled before, I knew how to roll around on the ground with another grown man without it being weird. I knew enough not to stick my fingers in someone's nose or put my opponent in a noogy headlock, which I saw a few times that day.

After everyone had their chance to get out there and get their bumps and bruises, we moved to the next drill. We all lined up, and then, one at a time, we had to fight our way through a gauntlet of team members holding big strike pads, the kind you might see at a football practice. Basically, everyone's job was to collectively beat the crap out of you as you fought your way to the other side, where your gun was sitting on the ground. The idea was that you should never quit fighting for your gun.

The gauntlet drill was not a lot of fun for a 145-pound guy like me. When it was my turn, I fought my way through the gauntlet to receive my beating, I mean training, and I somehow managed to stay on my feet. Suddenly, I felt my shoulder "pop" as someone hit me from the right side, just behind my shoulder blade. It was a full year before it felt normal again. I never said anything to anyone or reported it. I figured bumps and bruises were part of the deal. But I told myself if I was ever in charge of training, I wouldn't make people go through a gauntlet drill. Add that to my list, right next to spider drops.

I cannot even begin to estimate how many trainings I've attended over my career, but that particular day was one I'd remember more than most, because it showed us if you wanted to be able to protect yourself, you had to put work into it. Each of us had to get out there in front of everyone and use our physical skills against another person. I was never a "martial artist," but at least I had some experience and a little bit of coordination. I was skinny and unassuming, and most people didn't see me as a physical threat. I was perfectly okay with that, when I was in my guitar player mode. However, I wasn't okay with that when I put on a uniform, or when I was out on the shooting range. At times I had a bit of an attitude about that, and I'm sure it was why I was so motivated to put in whatever work it took to get better at it.

After training, I went home that night and researched the hunting dog story. I knew I was missing something there. I found out that the original analogy of that story came from a Cherokee legend, where a wise elder is speaking to a young boy about the inner battle all humans face. He tells the boy that the battle is like two wolves constantly fighting for dominance. They fight for control: love versus anger, envy versus charity, hate versus kindness, and humility versus arrogance. When the boy anxiously asks the wise elder, "But which wolf wins?" the elder responds, "The one that you feed."

Aha, I got it! The type of person you become is the type of person you "feed."

The next day the phone rang on my side of the yard at work. I picked it up and heard a familiar voice on the other end.

"Wanna feed the dog tonight?" It was my buddy Chris from the team, one of my best friends who later became a godparent to my children. Apparently, I wasn't the only one who was influenced by the story.

Of course, I wanted to feed the dog! At that time in my career, I was motivated to perfect every skill I was supposed to have. Mostly because of the SERT program, and because of trainings like the one we had just had, I saw the difference in attitude between those who were just getting by versus those who were striving to excel. I saw how those who were working the hardest seemed to stick out from the pack. They were the guys who never missed a day to work out. They were the guys who, instead of standing around bullshitting with their buddies at the range, chose to get in as much trigger time as possible.

Those were the guys who found every opportunity to train, and they loved the process of honing their craft. They were the guys you wanted to have around you if things went bad. I wanted to be like those guys.

Since Chris and I worked on the same yard, we started meeting up to train. At that time, he was a PTM, and I was the PTM drill instructor. More than a DI though, I was their trainer. On our regular jobs, we were both assigned to the third watch shift, which was from 1430 to 2230 hours.

Most nights, there was an hour at the end of the shift when things were usually quiet. All the inmates were locked up in their dorms, and the tier officers used that time to hand out mail or catch up on paperwork. While everyone else took care of their remaining duties for the shift, Chris and I used that time to feed the dog.

We'd meet up in the inmate barber shop and often stayed in there until it was time to go home. It was basically an office on the second tier that they tossed a couple of barber chairs in. We'd go in there and work on handcuffing, striking, blocking, or whatever else we could come up with. Sometimes we would take turns attacking each other so the other person could practice blocking the attack, countering, and then controlling their opponent to get handcuffs on them.

When another buddy from our team, Doug, who was also our yard sergeant, found out what we were up to, he started joining us. Not only was he one of our best friends, but he was also our boss. Training with the sergeant who was also your buddy was like having a pass to break things.

As we were running out of space, we started using the larger room next to the sergeant's office. We'd close the door so people couldn't see what we were doing, even though it was pretty obvious what was going on due to the banging around that took place behind that door. Like a group of young boys at grade school, there was also a lot of giggling when we broke something.

We loved training with Doug. We'd usually start training with just one move, thinking it would only take a minute or two. Then one move led to another, and before we knew it we would look up at the clock to realize the shift was over a long time ago. We'd sometimes walk out of the back room and notice everyone from our watch had already gotten off duty.

During the training sessions, things got progressively more and more hazardous, and the personal danger of each repetition steadily escalated. I loved having Doug with us because he was skinny like me. That meant I wasn't the only one who ended up recoiling in excruciating pain every once in a while. I don't know how many times I had to stop to hold some part of my body motionless until I was convinced it wasn't broken. We were usually forced to conclude the training not necessarily because it was time to go home, but due to an injury timeout.

At one point, the time we spent in the back room wasn't enough for us anymore, so we'd take it out to the parking lot after getting off duty. As usual, the training sessions would escalate if the previous drill hadn't hurt anyone too badly. That meant we continually turned things up a notch.

We would use whatever we had available to "attack" each other with it. First, we'd go hands vs hands. Then, hands vs feet. Then, someone pulled out an ASP baton from their car. Baton vs hands. Someone grabbed a stick off the ground. Baton vs stick. Then, stick vs hands. Then, stick vs feet. Every possible combination was used, until we saw what happened when you went head vs pavement. It was a good thing I was wearing a beanie hat that night, because I think it held my brains inside my head. That "lesson" left quite a knot, let me tell you.

We'd sometimes be training so late that one of our cell phones would ring as one of our wives wondered where the hell her husband was. Sometimes we'd still be out there training in the parking lot at 1:00 in the morning, and we had been off duty for two and a half hours.

I learned a lot from those training sessions, especially about how to work around your equipment. With a duty belt weighed down by a huge ring of Folger Adam keys, radio, baton, handcuffs, pepper spray and other equipment, the attacker had the advantage, at least until your partners showed up. That made it that much more important to train with that stuff on your waistline.

I tried as hard as I could to be a good partner, but I got a lot more out of those training sessions than Chris did. I was like an open book, and he had really good experience to share with me. Whether it was his experience in Kajukenbo or his Jujitsu from the Cesar Gracie School, I wanted to learn as much as I could from him. When we weren't at work, we would meet once a week at a small gym by his house where we would grapple, practice submissions, and work on striking focus mitts or strike pads. I loved it, especially when someone new joined in, because it was a way to see if what we were learning actually worked.

I really didn't think too much about those training sessions at the time, because it seemed normal to us. Looking back, I realize what we were doing wasn't normal. Not at all. While everyone else couldn't wait to get home, we stayed at the prison late, to hone our craft. We wanted to be the kind of guys you could count on if things went bad. We wanted that more than we wanted anything else.

By the end of my career, I will have spent twenty-three years in the California Department of Corrections, and I've heard so many officers complain about things in the department, especially the training. Sometimes, I had a really tough time listening to some of their complaints without getting irritated. Why? Because it is easy to complain, but finding a way to do something about it takes a lot of energy. It also takes a few bumps and bruises. I couldn't tell you how many times I conducted a training for officers, and then I'd later hear only the negatives.

The thing I learned from all our little "feed the dog sessions" was this: If something is important to you, go find a way to make it happen. If we had waited for someone else to schedule the training, or if we had tried to find a better venue than the barber shop upstairs, or if we had asked for permission to do it, none of it would have happened. Our department was a roadblock for things out of the ordinary. The amount of paperwork and necessary approvals usually meant it was a lot easier to ask for forgiveness than to ask for permission.

We never scoffed at any technique, prop or location. If we thought it might make us better, we found a way to use it. We also spent our own money and used our own vacation time to attend several training courses, getting into any course we could get into. We never asked the department to pay for those courses or to reimburse us for them. We simply enjoyed the experience of trying to get better, and we loved learning new methods and techniques.

I never really thought of myself as a tough guy, but in the process of training so hard, I had to be careful about developing a chip on my shoulder. I didn't really see it at the time, but looking back now it's pretty clear it was happening. We were training harder and more often than most people knew. I'd sometimes come to work with a black eye, or marks all over my face, but every bump and bruise was another important lesson I learned the hard way. I was proud of those lessons. Over time, those lessons begin to stack up, and if that is the dog you are feeding, you have to be careful not to let it get out of control. As I was becoming more able to handle myself in a confrontation, I found myself less likely to avoid them. After all, when the dog you are feeding is motivated by trouble, it tends to look out for it more.

I soon realized there was something more to the "feeding the dog" analogy than just some old legend, because I found myself experiencing the conflict within myself. I had the artistic, carefree dog who played the guitar on one side, and the harsher, more confrontational dog with an attitude on the other. They had both become important aspects of my life, so I tried to keep them independent from each other. The problem was, it was hard to feed both of them at the same time.

CHAPTER 11: TIER COP

Aside from CRT trainings, our everyday job involved whatever our regular assignment was at the prison. Just like for most SWAT teams from other agencies, shooting guns and training for hostage rescue wasn't our everyday job assignment – even though we wished it was.

There are a lot of possible assignments for a correctional officer. There are culinary officers, who are responsible for ensuring the kitchen and dining room areas are supervised and accounted for. Tower officers are posted in armed observation towers, and they overlook yards, sally ports and perimeter areas. Control booth officers regulate access into work areas and inmate housing buildings, and they might also issue equipment and keys. Officers who work lock-up units, such as the Administrative Segregation Unit (ASU), work in highly secure areas that house inmates who cannot live in the general population. There are also numerous medical assignments for officers, which might involve escorting inmates to and from appointments, supervising medication lines, or providing security in hospital areas. Of all the possible jobs a correctional officer might have, there was one I liked more than all others: I loved working the tier. Officers who ran a tier were called *tier cops*.

The California prison system has four housing levels, I-IV, from the lowest to highest in security needs. Our prison had

Level I, II and III units. The unit Chris, Doug and I worked on was a Level II, and it had around 1500 inmates who lived in 36-man dormitories. I loved working on that yard because it was such an interesting place to work. This had become quite the contrast to how I felt when I first joined the department. A lot of this had to do with my involvement in the SERT program, which had given me a lot of skills and an increased situational awareness that I used in my everyday job, which actually made the job more fun for me.

I loved working third watch (1430 to 2230 hours) because there was a lot of inmate activity to pay attention to. At that time of day as the evening was approaching, most of the inmate workers had returned from their work assignments, so the exercise yard was usually full. As you looked out across the yard, swarms of inmates were literally everywhere, playing handball, walking the track, working out, or just lulling around within their ethnic/prison gang groups. As a result of all those inmates out there, there was always some kind of drama to have to deal with, whether it was a disrespectful inmate, yard tension, or even the occasional fight or riot.

Since the yard we worked on had dorms, that provided an interesting dimension to supervising prison life. As a tier officer, you were assigned a section that had six or seven dorms. Since each dorm had 36 inmates in them at that time, it meant the ratio of inmates to tier officers was as high as 252:1. It wouldn't be easy to deal with 252 Franciscan nuns, much less inmates. But I loved it because no matter how frustrating it might be at times to work as a correctional officer, it was nice to get out there on your tier to just do your job, which was deal with inmates. That, to me, was the easiest part of the job.

I actually got along well with most inmates, except for the ones that caused trouble. Most inmates, at least on that particular yard, don't really cause much trouble, and some were actually pleasant to be around, but all it takes is one troublemaker. Some dorms had several. We sometimes saw the entire yard dynamic change with one inmate who showed up on the yard. It happened quite a few times.

A good tier officer knew his inmates. Some officers even knew every inmate in their section by name, aka, gang affiliation and what town or area they came from. The thing about working a tier was that you were surrounded by so many different personalities, so there was never a dull moment.

While on one hand it taught me that not all inmates are bad, it also taught me there are some extremely troubled individuals walking this earth. Some inmates were the type of people who cannot help but to cause trouble no matter where they go, and although they are far outnumbered by those who program, they cause the biggest disruptions.

Working on that yard also taught me a lot about enforcing rules. When I first started working the yard, I thought I should enforce all rules, as written. It was as if I had the bright white good guy cowboy hat, and all the inmates were the bad guys in black cowboy hats. It was like I was in some western, where the good guy was supposed to always do the right thing, and was always supposed to win in the end. It was me against the world, taking a bite out of crime, one troublemaker at a time.

I ended up exhausting myself. I enforced the rules on my tier and develop a "squared away" housing area, but as inmates came and went, I found myself chasing my tail. I'd get all my dorms to follow my program, and get them on board regarding how I liked my tier ran, but as the next batch of inmates showed up I'd find myself starting all over. It was then that I began to find out it was better for me to follow my heart, rather than a rule book. This didn't mean I would allow them to do whatever they wanted, but I came to the realization it was not my job to change them into better people or to punish them. The respect I got on the yard immediately changed and became much more genuine, because the inmates began to see me as "fair" rather than "strict". It was a lesson I would keep with me from that point forward, especially as I later became a supervisor of my own yard.

Since our prison was pretty old, the dorms were smelly, ugly, and noticeably decomposing. When you walked into a dorm, paint could be seen coming off the walls, and electrical panels were usually twisted back or broken, providing inmates neat little hiding places for their stashes of whatever it was they wanted to hide. The maintenance department would sometimes shut down an entire dorm while they tried to renovate it, but it was impossible to keep up with the deterioration of the yard.

Going into a dorm is like walking into the wrong neighborhood, as everyone living there takes notice and wonders what you are up to. It's the responsibility of the first inmate who sees you to announce "Walking!" when you enter. That way all the other inmates know you're present. If you saw someone scurry to hide their tattoo guns or other paraphernalia, you only had to walk up and ask them to step away from their bunk. Then you took a look under their blanket or behind the pillow or under the mattress, and there you might find – and immediately confiscate – a cell phone, a tattoo gun, tobacco, or whatever else it was they were trying to hide. Bad inmate. You might even find drugs or a weapon, although they are usually sly enough to wait until the middle of the night to mess with that stuff. Routine searching minimizes the presence of contraband, but since the troublemakers have all day and night to conjure up ways to find it, make it, or stash it, it was a constant battle to control it.

At count time, the inmates were all sent back to their living areas so officers could walk through and count everyone. I enjoyed that time of the shift because I saw it as such a fascinating aspect of civilization, and I knew it was something most people didn't get to see. All those inmates, from every conceivable background and upbringing, whether they were black, white, Hispanic or some other ethnicity, and whether they were from inner-cities, or from out in the country, or from rich neighborhoods, trailer parks or even from under the bridge in a tent down by the river, all locked up together in one housing unit. As you walked into the dorm, you looked around and found yourself surrounded by gang-bangers, drug dealers, car thieves, burglars, and every other conceivable criminal type. How do you deal with that? At first, you pretend like it's nothing to you. As you walk through the dorm, you feel 72 eyeballs staring at you, silently, watching every move you make, and then you find a way to shrug it off and just do your job. It gets easier each time you do it, and then before you know it, it feels not much different than walking into the supermarket down the road. I always wondered if the moment when it became no longer weird to be inside a dorm was the moment when there was no return of normalcy for you.

Correctional officers are an interesting group of people, because of what they see and what they deal with every day. It is an environment where you cannot afford to look weak, yet overcompensating and being a total asshole often ends up effecting everyone else around you, including your partners. Plus, acting like an asshole all the time will probably bleed over to your regular life eventually, and you might end up treating regular people out there the same way. I don't think it is possible to do that job and not have it effect how you see the world. I think the bigger challenge is to be able to do the job without having it effect how you *treat* the world. One thing for certain is once you get used to working inside a prison, there isn't much that happens out in the world that surprises you anymore. The job tends to give you a changed opinion of what "normal" is.

Of all the things to not like about being inside a dorm, my least favorite thing about being a tier officer was during the flu season, when you could practically see the germs floating around in the air as inmates coughed, sneezed and farted when you walked through. There were times I had to hold my breath as I walked through the dorm, especially as I reached the bathroom area. The truth is, books and movies often attempt to depict what life is like within a prison housing unit, but it is often more entertaining than even what Hollywood portrays it to be.

To me, life within the dorms resembled some type of human sociology experiment as the inmates found a way to coexist with each other. There were formal, documented departmental rules they were supposed to follow, and there were unwritten rules they chose to enforce in their own ways. They pretty much do what they can to keep the peace, but when you have so many people in such a close proximity to each other, there are going to be problems. When someone does something that violates their own set of rules, it causes tension. The fact that inmates set up their own rules is kind of interesting, considering that some of them have been breaking rules their entire lives. They just don't want *you* breaking *their* rules.

Tension in the dorm is usually the result of someone doing something that affects the livelihood of other inmates. Inmates like consistency, and if someone starts causing problems, they're going to be dealt with. That means either relocating that inmate to another dorm or him getting beaten up. At times, the beating is a chin check or maybe a really nice shiner, but at times the recipient of the beating ends up fighting for their life in intensive care. It all depends on what they did. It also depends on how overzealous the attackers get. Some of them are not known for their self-control.

When you walk through a dorm and there is tension, it is not a good feeling. You can tell, just by the overall inmate body language, that something either happened or is going to happen. There is nothing like standing there in the middle of a bunch of inmates and knowing something is wrong. A fight between inmates could involve the entire dorm. On occasion, multiple dorms can go off at the same time, which is a tough situation to deal with. You are definitely not going home anytime soon when that happens, because there are going to be inmates, clothing and property scattered all over the place to deal with.

There is also the possibility of inmates using a weapon to make a statement, which became more and more prevalent even on our Level I and II yards. It never ceased to amaze me how some inmates would basically throw their life away, sometimes when they only had a few months left to do.

I think one of the main reasons I loved being a tier officer was because it reminded me of how good I had it. When you think you have house trouble, or car trouble, or bill trouble, or life trouble, all you need to do is walk through an inmate housing unit, and you will realize your problems are really not that bad.

While walking the tier, I couldn't help but notice how inmates occupied themselves with the simplest of things. They pass the time playing cards, reading a book, flipping through a magazine, or listening to music through their headphones. Every Friday, I would walk through my dorms one last time before going home, and I'd notice how content a lot of the inmates looked lying on their bunks with a book in their hands. I couldn't wait to get home and enjoy a book of my own, or just pick up my guitar and shut the rest of the world off for a bit. Sometimes our lives are so busy that we forget to take a moment to enjoy the simplest of things, and in a strange way, being a tier officer often reminded me of that.

CHAPTER 12: BLINDSIDED

I was standing in my driveway when I realized my first marriage was over. What's crazy is that I had to find it out from my dogs.

"I'm surprised," I said. "She usually lets the dogs in before it gets dark."

"They've been out there barking every night, for almost two weeks," my neighbor replied.

"Well, maybe she's been working a little late."

"At ten at night?"

I searched for an answer. I didn't have one.

"Hey, man," he said nervously. "I hope I'm not getting anyone in trouble or anything. I have to tell you, though, your wife hasn't been coming home until around ten, maybe ten-fifteen every night. It's been obvious, because your dogs are outside barking constantly until she comes home to let them in."

Four and a half hours is a long time for a neighbor to have to listen to someone's dogs bark. I can imagine what it must have sounded like, because those two dogs were big babies. If they noticed the sun going down, they'd start barking, and they would not stop until you let them inside. They barked because they wanted to remind you that they were supposed to be inside, where it is safe and cozy.

I had a feeling something was wrong. It's one of those things you can't put your finger on, but you know something is not right. It was a bunch of little things, like a few things she had said, a name from work that seemed to come up more than normal, or even an email I caught a glimpse of that she covered before I could finish reading. Normally, it wouldn't be that big of a deal if she came home late, but the fact that it was every night, and she was staying out until just moments before I was coming home from my shift, well, hearing this felt like getting punched right in the stomach. My neighbor could see it too, all over my face.

I'm not making anyone out to be the bad guy, because I take just as much blame. I was preoccupied. I was in love with my training. I didn't want to miss out on anything, so I was gone a lot. I never turned down an opportunity to go to a training or to a certification course, and if there was any kind of a team activation, I would grab my gear and run in to work, because I loved being with the guys. Although I may have had a gut feeling that something was wrong in our relationship, I was too preoccupied to actually see it, until it was too late.

I decided to go inside to ask her about it. Maybe there was an explanation. When I told her the neighbor had complained about our dogs being outside so late, she stared at me across the kitchen with absolutely nothing to say. She didn't have to say anything. She moved out by the end of the week.

At first, I was devastated. It was a tough thing to get through because I loved being married. We never really discussed having children or starting a family and, in a sense, it was like we were still dating, except we were living in the same house with the same last name. We went out to expensive dinners, took trips, went on scuba diving vacations, and even took the dogs camping with us, just like we were a nice, happy family. Having dogs though, is not really like having kids, and people who think it is the same thing have no idea. Our relationship was not moving forward, especially when it came to whether or not we were going to have children, and this was mostly because we were both too caught up in our own careers. When she moved out, I suddenly realized the thing I was missing in my life was a family. I wondered if I had blew it, by living like we were still dating.

At the time, I was playing music in a little three-piece band, and I remember the odd look they both gave me after they had asked how things were going. It was obvious something was wrong. As we were breaking things down after a band rehearsal, I told them that the thing I worried most about was getting through life and not knowing what it was like to hold your newborn in your arms. Do real dudes ever say things like that to other dudes? I don't know, but it just came out, and they both looked at me weird, almost like it was pity.

I couldn't help it though. I wanted a wife. I wanted kids. I wanted family vacations and Thanksgiving and Christmas and Disneyland and homework and yelling and toys scattered all around the house. I wanted to totally dork out with all of it. Yes, the idea of remaining single the rest of my life, with nice sports cars, expensive sunglasses and total freedom to do whatever I wanted did appeal to me, but the idea of having a family seemed cooler to me.

Once I started dating again, I realized how much I hated it. You'd think a decent looking guy with a good job, no children, and nothing tying him down would have a good time being out there in the dating scene. I didn't. I could not believe how many people out there have issues and baggage.

I even tried online dating, because it was convenient, but it was *too* convenient. I preferred meeting girls the old-fashioned way, where you walked up to them at the supermarket, gas station or bookstore and actually introduced yourself. Social media and the internet made dating weird, and much too deceptive.

With people using profile pictures taken ten years earlier and their 100-item list of characteristics they need in a lover, I sometimes felt like I was applying for a job instead of a date. It felt so fake. Plus, I wasn't comfortable having my picture online on a dating service due to my job. That made it harder to meet people, because I had to explain why I didn't have a photo on my profile.

I remember my very first date after the divorce. I met a girl online who definitely did not have a large mole on her cheek in her profile pictures. I honestly wouldn't even have cared about the mole, but when I met her, I couldn't help but wonder if her profile photos were doctored.

We met for Mexican food and then went to a bar for a drink. After that, she asked me if I wanted to go back to her place. *Okay*, I'm thinking, *online dating is really easy*. I agreed, and we hung out and watched a movie. I don't even remember what movie it was, maybe because we didn't get five minutes into the movie before the possibility of things getting beyond first base became apparent. To be honest, I was mostly interested in just getting back into the dating scene and meeting different people. I wasn't ready for anything serious, and I certainly didn't think I'd already be sitting on someone's couch wondering if having sex was going to make it all the better or all the worse.

I realized I wanted to go home more than I wanted to stay. My mind was not right yet because the divorce still weighed on my mind, and I didn't want to feel like I was supposed to call someone the next day. I told her I had to be going since I had to work the next morning. When I stood up, she moved in close and put her arms around me. That's when I told myself I was thinking way too much about all this. There was nothing wrong with being affectionate with someone. Plus, after all, I was single now.

I let the hug and the rubbing proceed. *Ah, this ain't so bad,* I thought. Then, as we got ready to kiss, which would be my first kiss since the divorce, and our cheeks passionately slid by each other, something scraped right along the side of my face. *My God*, I thought. *Was that her mole?* I didn't take that very well, so I went home. I realized dating was not going to be easy for me, because I suddenly wondered how I was supposed to know if someone was right for me.

I wasn't interested in future dates if I didn't see things going anywhere. I wasn't interested in friends with benefits, or booty calls or people with baggage. I wasn't interested in just getting laid. While some guys go through their divorce and rebel by working out, dying their hair, and then having sex with as many women as possible, I really didn't want extra drama, or diseases, in my life. I hated trying to keep track of who I was supposed to see each weekend, and if I was on a date with one girl and another one called me, I felt like I was cheating. For me, it wasn't as much fun as it sounds like to married guys. Plus, dating gets really *expensive*.

Of course, there is always dating someone from work. However, it is a really bad idea. I wouldn't recommend it. The risk is too great, and when things don't work out, or if they end badly, it makes things weird at work. I saw it too many times, and I did what I could to avoid it. Actually, I dated someone from work, but only once. And I'm glad my attempts to avoid it eventually failed.

On our first date, Jody and I went to San Francisco, which was a two-hour drive from my house. I had been to the city countless times before, but that particular visit would be my most memorable one ever. It was a typical, chilly San Francisco evening. I knew of a few spots that overlooked the city lights, so after dinner we drove around to find them. We parked at each spot and got out of my truck to check out the view. As we stood there admiring the awesome San Francisco skyline, we enjoyed each other's company.

Without a doubt, she is one of the funniest people you could ever meet, which anyone who meets her recognizes immediately. Her sense of humor is contagious, but there was another side of her personality that really caught me off-guard. She not only had a strong, infectious sense of faith, but her views on the world were also intelligent as well as passionate. She was unwavering in her beliefs yet refused to corner herself into one stereotypical political ideology. That made her really fun and engaging to talk to.

As we drove around the city, I couldn't help but to sometimes look over at her in the passenger seat. I'd think to myself how she was going to be an awesome wife for someone. *How in the hell is this girl not married?* Of all the dates I had been on, I never saw someone in that kind of light. I also never thought about what kind of mom someone would be, but Jody was different. She just had that thing about her, like it was what she was destined to be.

She had it all. She was good looking, funny, smart, and more than anything else, I could not imagine wanting to date or see anyone else. I was totally blindsided on that very first date. I was more nervous than I'd ever been in my life.

Soon, she became all I could think about. We talked every day. We tried to take things slow, but it was hard because I wanted to hang out with her all the time. Both of us went out on other dates, but I would even call her on the way home, just because I loved talking to her so much. Eventually, I realized I was in love, and to be honest, I know it started on that very first date.

I proposed to her on a quiet, tiny little tucked-away beach on Maui. I had it all planned out after we decided to go on vacation there. I was hiding the ring throughout the entire vacation. First, I thought the X-ray people at the airport were going to give it up. As they were scanning my bag, back and forth, back and forth, a couple of them gathered around the screen. I figured they saw something and were going to have me empty my bag on the table. Luckily, they smiled and told me to have a nice vacation instead. After the first moment of anxiousness was over, I had to keep it hidden, and I was deathly afraid of losing it. I must have peeked into my bag a thousand times during that trip.

    I rented a jeep so we could drive all the way around the island. The road to Hana has a lot of really cool stops along the way. We'd stop, jump out, snap a picture, and then we'd hop back into the rental to be off again. I'm sure Jody was wondering why the hell we were in such a hurry. She had to be thinking I was crazy. For me, it wasn't a sightseeing expedition as much as a recon for the perfect spot to propose. My goal was to do it at sunset, and that meant marking down on a map all the places I liked and then getting back to the perfect spot before the sun went down.

    I ended up proposing to her on some tiny beach off the road that was surrounded by palm trees. It was a cool little spot, and if you weren't looking really hard for it, you might drive right by. I was in such a hurry to get us there before the sun went down. I grabbed her hand and quickly hopped over the railing to hustle down to the sand. By that time, she was probably ready to spend the rest of her vacation with someone who wasn't a spaz. I took a deep breath and proposed while the sun was sinking into the Pacific Ocean.

CHAPTER 13: THE CHAIR

There is a chair I know of that is placed very strategically, but it has the most humble of appearances. It is a great chair, though. You'd think a chair of importance would be more elegant, considering it marks the most significant moments of life. It should be throne-like, with gold and silver and shiny stuff all over it. There should be feather-wavers standing alongside it, serving the one who sits there. Instead, its fabric is made of an uninspiring shade of 60s blue. The legs are old and bent, so they don't really touch the ground at the same angles, causing it to wiggle as you sit on it.

The first time I sat in that chair, I gave my life away.

My wife was quickly wheeled into the room behind the swinging doors. A nurse informed me that I would need to wait there, right in that chair, and to not worry. They were going to do an emergency cesarean because the heart rate of the baby had disappeared.

My world spun uncontrollably as I sat down on that chair. There was a tiny little human in there that we were so excited to meet, and now I didn't even know if that was going to happen. I thought back nine months earlier when Jody showed me her pregnancy stick. I cried when I saw the little blue lines because I was so excited to be a daddy. We had gone through two miscarriages, one of which was at twenty weeks. That was brutal for us both.

When we got to the hospital earlier that day, they put us in a room and hooked her to all the little monitor devices. The little "whoosh, whoosh" of a baby's heartbeat was a soothing sound that we were very familiar with. The sound we were not familiar with was the horrifying, steady "Beeeeeeeeeee!" It was just like in the movies, but a lot worse in real life. Nurses rushed in frantically, and they started rolling Jody around on the bed to try to get the baby righted in her tummy.

There is one thing you notice about going to the hospital: nurses do not look worried. They are usually cool as a cucumber as they go about their duties, because they have seen and dealt with just about everything. Let me tell you something I learned that day about nurses. They look very fucking worried when there is a little baby whose heart rate has just disappeared.

They quickly wheeled Jody out of the room, right across the way into the delivery room. There were quite a few mothers there that morning, waiting to deliver their babies too, but situations like this give you priority. As she was wheeled out of our room, we looked at each other, and I will never forget the expression on her face. *No, not again. Not now.*

Jody is a woman who wanted nothing more in life than to be a mommy, just as I knew on that very first date. It is what she was meant to be. But right then, it seemed that it was being taken from her once again. Our nurses looked really concerned, and as they wheeled her out of the room, one of them basically *shouted at* me.

"Kiss her right *now*. Tell her that you love her!"

Jody's hospital bed almost rammed into another incoming bed as they pushed her out into the hallway. As I looked at the person lying on that other bed, I noticed it was Lisa, the pregnant wife of my best friend and training partner, Chris. We had agreed that we were going to be the godparents for each other's babies. Even though they lived over a hundred miles away, they were rushed to this particular hospital by ambulance because their baby was suddenly having complications. It was totally random, as Chris and Lisa were not ever even planning to deliver their baby in that particular hospital, and their baby was not due for weeks.

My world was spinning too much at the time to be thinking about how coincidental it all was. Chris threw his arms around me and just held me for a moment, and I could only sob, as the emotions overtook me. I'm not sure if he had any idea what to say, because what do you say to someone in this situation? But the words that came out of his mouth were perfect: the Lord's Prayer. I said it along with him, but my voice was shaking. Somehow, it calmed me down, and I went out to go sit in that rickety blue chair outside the delivery room.

From where I sat, I could see through the windows of the large double doors. Doctors and nurses hurriedly covered their faces with masks. I closed my eyes and started praying.

"If you are in need of a life up there in heaven, please, just take mine instead. Give this baby to her mommy," I said.

With every passing year, I watch Madeline grow taller and taller and more and more beautiful. I am continually amazed at her as she is quickly turning into a woman. She gave us quite a scare on that day. She had to spend a week in the NICU before we were finally able to take her home. I will never forget that I owe her my life. I plan to give it to her, every single day of it.

The second time I sat in the chair, my mind raced uncontrollably again. It was that very same blue chair in that very same location. A nurse came out from the room behind the double doors and softly told me it was time to go inside. I entered the room and cautiously walked up to Jody, who was half-covered by a large white sheet.

I could hear the low murmuring of Dr. Henry, who also delivered Madeline, as he worked to do God-knows-what on the other side of that sheet. I didn't want to know. As they pulled and pushed, Jody's upper body was shifting back and forth. She looked over at me and whispered, "I love you," and then vomited into a blue bag.

The next sound I heard was the most amazing sound in the existence of all mankind. It was a beautiful, soft cry as it echoed throughout the room for that very first time. Hearing it sent both of us into a chorus of happy tears. It would only seem like a blink of an eye before that very same little handsome voice would walk up to his mother to say, "Mommy, you are the most beee-youuu-tee-full mommy in the hoe-wide world." Wyatt was handsome and sweet on that very first day, and from that point forward, he only got more so.

The third time I sat in that chair, I witnessed something completely amazing. After they walked me through those same large double doors, they led me up to Jody, who was smiling and lying down on what I assume was that very same delivery bed. I walked up to her and kissed her, and I noticed how absolutely beautiful she looked. She still had that glow to her that pregnant women have, and even more so at that moment.

They pushed and pulled at her lower half and even asked me if I wanted to look over the blanket to watch. I didn't get to see the last two times, so I slowly peeked over the sheet to immediately realize, *Nah, it's all good*. I recoiled back to my side of the sheet and tried not to show any disgust on my face.

"What does it look like over there?" Jody asked me.

"I think there is a baby in there somewhere."

Within seconds, Dr. Henry lifted up the baby in the air and cheerfully announced, "It's a boy!" They cleaned our little Walker up and then handed him to Jody. As I watched the two of them, I realized the most amazing bond in the world is the bond that exists between mother and her child. I found myself totally captivated watching the two of them. I remember thinking to myself how those two amazing humans deserve each other.

They handed me little Walker and told me they were going to patch Jody up. They led the two of us out to that very same blue chair in that very same spot, and they told me to hang out there with the baby for a few minutes. I sat down in that blue chair and held that little boy, and I had to try hard to focus through my watery eyes. I was amazed at every yawn and twitch he made.

The nurses and staff gave us our space, and even though we were in a hospital with all its noise and commotion, we found ourselves in complete silence and solitude, as if we were the only two people on earth. I watched with astonishment as he struggled to open his eyes for that very first time. His very first sight in life was me staring into his eyes. I whispered to him the first thing that came to mind.

"Hey, there. I'm your daddy. And I will never let you down, ever."

I plan on keeping that promise, let me tell you.

The next time I sat in the chair I knew it would be my last. Jody and I had talked things over, and we agreed this would be our last baby, mostly because it would be Jody's fourth cesarean. Dr. Henry delivered the next little Sharkey baby into the world, and after cleaning her up, the nurses placed little Abigail on Jody's chest. I watched them in amazement, and I thought that love can never be explained sufficiently by science and cells. There is more to it than that. A nurse then handed Abigail over to me, so they could prepare Jody for the recovery room. The nurse walked Abigail and me outside to that same old blue chair, one last time.

I sat there, holding her and staring into that angelic face, and I fell head over heels in love. Sitting in that familiar blue chair, right there in the middle of that birthing center, I did the first thing that came to mind. I sang to her. The only song I could think of was *Farewell and Adieu,* an old sailors' shanty the kids and I heard from one of our all-time favorite movies, *Jaws*.

It's the song Quint, the swarthy shark catcher, sings to give calmness to even the most turbulent of scenes. It is a ballad that was once sung by sailors as they lifted anchor to head back home.

Abigail stared calmly into my face as I sung to her, as if she knew what I was singing about. Not long after that, her first word would be her own name, "Abaga!" That should tell you how much we spoiled her. How could you not spoil that little thing, especially when her most common phrase would later be, "Mommy, you are the best mommy EVER!"?

See, I knew it. Right from that first date.

CHAPTER 14: AMAZING GRACE

As they waited, I hope they felt the same way we did. I hope they tried to not seem nervous as they looked around the room to figure out how bad it was going to be. I hope one of them started stretching, and the others realized it was a good idea. I hope they checked their watches and occasionally glanced out the window expecting a storm to come in. It was all part of the deal.

The morning of tryouts was something I didn't want them to forget. I wanted it to be one of those days that changed their career – provided that they were looking for more purpose in the job.

When it came to being a drill instructor, I only knew of one kind. Every drill instructor I had ever met in my life was an asshole. They were mean, nasty, loud, and a bit crazy. My partner, Dave, was a great partner in crime, because just like me, he could be mean, nasty, loud, and a bit crazy. Also, both of us felt an overwhelming obligation to do the job right. I'm not sure if they realized what they were getting when they paired us together. If you wanted the new guys to be tested, we were the right guys for that the job. We loved playing that role.

I didn't realize how much it would take out of me, though. Playing the bad guy takes a lot of energy. You are constantly correcting, motivating, disciplining, inspiring and encouraging. You have to find the right time to do each – it is a delicate balance. You sometimes get it right, while other times you question yourself.

At first, you are just mean, because that is all you know. Then, from experience, you learn to make sure everything has a purpose. There has to be a method to the madness. When they are tired, you find energy. When they are frustrated, you find patience. When they are confused, you find solutions. Your job is to make them dig deep and believe they can get through anything together. We weren't the Army, or the Marines, or Navy SEALS, or anything like that, but we knew what it felt like to trust your partners, and we wanted them to know what that felt like too.

We told ourselves we would be able to do everything we asked them to do. No exceptions. That meant we had to stay on top of our game, whether it was shooting skills or physical condition. It was exhausting, because during training, we made sure there was absolutely no downtime and every single moment had an objective. We never did stupid shit that didn't have a purpose related to our mission. It really isn't too difficult to make people quit if that is your goal. We didn't want to make them quit. We wanted them to strive to be better.

Thinking back to First Sergeant Stanley and other leaders I met in my life, I adopted that style because I wanted to weed out those who didn't really want it. I didn't want to waste anyone's time. What they probably never realized, though, was that I saw so much potential in all of them, and usually it was more than what they may have seen in themselves.

Dave and I would end up training several groups of PTMs together over the years, and I think the first group suffered the worst of it. It was my "maiden voyage" as a drill instructor. They started calling my episodes with them "shark attacks," not only because of my last name but because of how brutal the sessions were. There was a different level of energy I found during those trainings and a different level of hunger. When I put them through those "shark attack" sessions, I was never mad at them, but they probably thought I was.

My wrath was never actually at them as much as the world. I'd think about being mediocre, or lazy, or slothful, and I'd get pissed off. I'd think about our haters, our naysayers, our cynics and our skeptics, and some of the people who tried to discredit the CRT team, and I'd get a fire under my ass. Don't even get me started on crappy leadership or micromanagement we saw in our regular jobs. I was never pissed off at the PTMs, but when I went into DI mode, I used whatever was available to get fired up.

Looking back now, I wonder if it's healthy to get all worked up like that. It can't be. No way. It did get easier to go into that role over time, because you realized it was only a part of a much bigger picture. Once they reach a certain point of proficiency, you take off those training wheels and treat them as teammates.

My favorite moment of tryouts was at the end of the day, and I always added the same little ritual. Whatever their assumptions may have been about what tryouts would be, I wanted to make sure they clearly saw what the CRT program was truly about. It had to be a total contrast from the department they once thought they knew.

As they pushed through on the final run up the hill, they were usually struggling to stay together. It isn't the largest of hills, but it feels pretty tough after the day they had just gone through. At the top of the hill is the SERT house, which was our locker room and staging area. The regular team members already headed back up there earlier to wait for the PTMs. As the PTMs approached the top of the hill, the bagpipe version of *Amazing Grace* was played on a loudspeaker.

The song is beautiful, humbling and haunting, especially for anyone who wears a uniform. I liked playing that song at the end of tryouts. Although it certainly has a religious significance to a lot of us, there is also a solemn feeling it invokes due to its tradition at the funerals of fallen heroes. The song reminds us of the responsibility people choose to accept when they put on a uniform and swear to protect others. As a correctional officer, we are not often portrayed as people who think this way, even though there are so many of us that actually do.

In our CRT culture, the song is revered, because it represents heroism, brotherhood, and all the things in life that separate good from evil. As we all stand in silence waiting for the song to end, the values of the CRT program should become very clear to everyone standing there. It also gives everyone a moment to consider their own personal values and to think about what is most important in their own lives.

It is impossible to not experience some level of emotion as *Amazing Grace* plays at the end of tryouts. It doesn't matter if you're the commander, a team member or a PTM. Over the years, I saw a lot of people standing there who had trouble holding back tears. I don't know what was ever on their minds, and I never asked. They were likely thinking about the things that were most important to them – whatever that was. Maybe it was their wife at home. Maybe it was their kids. Maybe both. Maybe they were thinking about how someday their son or daughter would look up to them as a hero. Maybe they were suddenly more proud of themselves than they had ever been before. They suddenly found a purpose beyond what they had expected when they first applied for the job.

We all need those moments in life when we are reminded of what is most important to us. Those moments reveal who we truly are. I became such a completely different person once I became a father. The world was a totally different place from the moment the nurse walked out to me sitting on that old blue chair, and told me both my wife and my brand-new daughter were okay.

As *Amazing Grace* plays at the end of all tryouts, I'm thinking about my wife and my kids. It becomes impossible to resist the tears that swell from behind my sunglasses, and it happens every single time. I stand there in that moment, and know if it weren't for my family, nothing in the world would mean much to me. If it weren't for those little humans who run up to me every single time I walk through the doorway to jump all over me and yell, "Daddyyyyyyyy," I wouldn't know how it felt to love someone on this Earth more than you love the air that you breathe.

As the tryout day concluded, there in our little CRT corner of the universe, we quietly waited for *Amazing Grace* to conclude. It is at that moment that you find out what things are most important in your life. It ends up being much, much more than simply joining a SWAT team.

CHAPTER 15: THE ROAD LESS TRAVELED

"Hey Sharkman," I hear from behind me. "How much farther?"

"About two clicks."

"Two clicks? That's what you said last time."

"I know that's what I said… It's about two clicks away."

Doug walked up closer, so nobody else could hear. Under his breath he said, "You can tell me, buddy. We're lost, right? Do you even know where we are?"

"Of course, I know where we are, Doug," I spurted. "We're about two clicks away."

In the military, we used a "click" for a 1,000-meter measurement. Since the maps in the Army had grid marks at 1,000-meter squares, knowing how many "clicks" you had to travel gave you a good estimate of distance. I figured "two clicks" never sounded all that bad. It wasn't too close, but it wasn't too far. The truth of the matter was I didn't want to tell them how far we really had to go, because then they would start having questions, and I didn't have the energy to answer questions. It was like being in a packed minivan on a long vacation. Are we there yet? Are we there yet? How much farther? Did you take a wrong turn? How much longer? Please tell us... are we there yet?

When we decided to participate in the High Sierra SWAT challenge, I was to become our navigator. I was decent at reading a map and using a compass, because we had to know how to do it back in the military. I also had a GPS to verify our position, but at that time, only expensive military-style GPSs provided as many details as they do now. As a result, I did most of our navigation by use of a compass and topographical map. That meant I spent more time staring into a map than actually looking around at the beautiful scenery around us. It also meant the guys were constantly looking over my shoulder to ask how far we still had to go.

The High Sierra SWAT Challenge took place in the mountains of the Kirkwood Ski Resort area near Lake Tahoe. It involved a trek through 63 miles of rugged terrain in the Eldorado National Forest, where each SWAT team who entered would have to navigate to each of the 21 checkpoints. At each checkpoint, teams would run through a scenario involving hostage rescue, high-risk warrant service, terrorist activity, weapons of mass destruction, rappelling, and other problem-solving scenarios. Teams had about 54 hours to get through the entire course, which meant we had to be on the move continuously with no sleep, hiking up and down elevations varying between 7,000 and 10,000 feet.

Before we even started training for the competition, the one thing we all agreed on was "absolutely no shortcuts." That meant not trying to cut across forested or mountainous areas as we were navigating between checkpoints. It is always better to stay on the trail if possible. Throughout the SWAT competition, we held strongly to this pact, until about a day and a half into it.

Even though our trail came to a sharp ninety-degree bend to the right, we thought, *Hmm, weird. The map shows our next checkpoint over there to the left, just over that teeny-weenie little mountain.* Screw the agreement, let's take The Road Less Traveled. Like the poem says, it might make all the difference in the world.

We were all really excited to be able to take part in this SWAT competition. When you work in a prison, you often feel cut off and alienated from the outside world, especially as a peace officer. After all, many agencies had trouble seeing us as peace officers, and that was a point of contention for us. Participating in a SWAT competition with so many other teams would give us a chance to get out there to see how we stacked up with other law enforcement agencies. It would give us a chance to see if our tactics were as effective as what others were using. In our hearts, we were just as good as any of those teams, and we felt because of the history of the SERT program, and the heart we all had to show to get through the training, there was nothing they could throw at us that would phase us. That's why when we looked at the trail going right, and then saw one little mountain to traverse if we went to the left, none of us thought twice about it. Screw the trail.

The thing about a mountain is that it looks a lot different when you are standing back looking at it. When you are trying to climb over it, you get to experience how every crest looks like it is the last one, but it isn't. At some point, it feels like there will *never* be a last crest, because it keeps going up and up and up. Two of the guys on our team could barely even walk, because they had massive chafing and foot issues. Trying to get over that mountain was ridiculously hard, and we were all hurting, so much that it was hard to walk. When you're in that kind of discomfort, and you're that tired, weird stuff happens. You start to hear and see things. People also get snappy.

"Damn! We should have taken that *road* right there to the top!"

"There's no road. It's a trail, and it doesn't go to the top. If you remember, we didn't take the trail."

"Bullshit! There's a road *right there*!"

"No, there isn't a road."

"Yes there is, dumbass. There is a road to the top. Right there. How else did they get that fucking RV up there?"

"That's not an RV, dumbass. That's a big white *rock*."

"No shit? Oh, never mind then."

Trekking up over that mountain would end up being the most difficult thing I'd done over the course of my career. Of all the challenges I had to face, going back to tryouts, the SERT academy, tough trainings and anything else I've had to endure, this was the hardest. Although it was more like some kind of grueling adventure race than a SWAT competition, grinding through such a difficult undertaking together was not foreign to us. After all, our tryouts to join the team involved an experience that felt, in many ways, quite similar to the grind of getting through this together. As we slowly made our way up to the top, there was a long moment where nobody said a word. As the scent of the surrounding pine trees accompanied each panting breath, I thought of how I never could have imagined I'd be doing something like this as a correctional officer. I loved the part of my job that was CRT, especially when it involved being away from the prison.

As our next checkpoint came into view, we noticed it was a medical checkpoint. Perfect. As we walked into the large tent, there were cots lined up and medical staff present to check on everyone. Aaron peeled his shoes off, because he needed a nurse to look at his feet. When she glanced down at his mangled feet she actually yelled, "Oh my Gaawwd!" The doctor in the medical team came over to take a look, stopping himself mid-step to go back to put on a pair of gloves before he touched Aaron's feet.

As everyone was getting patched up, I closed my eyes on a cot and thought about getting in a quick nap. I was exhausted, and we still had a long way to go. Instead of falling asleep though, I leaned over and grabbed the map to study it. I knew the guys were relying on me to get us to our next checkpoint, and to me, the worst thing I could ever do would be to let those guys down. It was my job to get us there, so I was going to study the shit out of that map every chance I had. Doug saw me reading the map and leaned over towards me.

"Hey buddy. How much farther to the next checkpoint?"

"Two clicks," I said, without looking up. From the corner of my eye, I saw him grinning as he leaned back into his cot.

When we left the medical checkpoint, I took a position up front to navigate to our next checkpoint, while everyone else filed behind. It was obvious everyone still hurt. We must have been quite a sight, up front erect and eager to proceed, while towards the back of our conga line, Aaron could barely walk and looked all hunched over like a caveman. We looked like the "March of Progress" drawing of evolution.

At the end of the competition, I lay down and was so tired I couldn't fall sleep. It was like my body was in shock. I thought about all the times in my life when I was tired, and this was a different kind of tired. When I finally drifted off to sleep, I dreamt of being back out on the course going to our next checkpoint. It wasn't a dream, it was a nightmare.

The High Sierra SWAT challenge eventually converted into Urban Shield, a massive 48-hour training exercise in the Bay Area. We would end up participating in Urban Shield, as well as other SWAT multi-agency trainings, and it always made me very proud to be able to participate in them. The SERT/CRT program was proving to be a highly respected SWAT program within our state, at least among the agencies we trained with. I enjoyed taking part in those trainings because I felt as if we were out there representing our department in a positive way, and in the process of that maybe doing something to establish some legitimacy and credibility for our department. It was something that mattered to us, and we were proud to be part of something like that.

I missed out on one year of Urban Shield because Wyatt, our second child, was due to be born the week after the event. As much as I wanted to be part of it, I couldn't have imagined not being there to watch the birth of my child. I couldn't risk it. The blue chair was waiting. Looking back at the memories I have, doing SWAT things was always a cool thing to be part of, but nothing is as cool as holding your child moments after they are born. When I didn't hesitate to exclude myself from such a major, international SWAT event, it was a clear indicator regarding where my priorities in life rested.

Of all the SWAT competitions, mutual trainings, and even large-scale search warrant operations we participated in, the High Sierra SWAT challenge was my favorite multi-agency event that we participated in, and it is because of our trek over that mountain. It was our way of showing that we were not afraid to go left while everyone else went right. Had we not taken a left turn at that mountain, we would have just been like every other SWAT team that year. Truth be told, none of us ever saw ourselves as like anyone else anyways, and maybe that was because we always felt like we had something to prove. I know none of us will ever forget going up over that mountain. I bet if you were to ask any of us if we'd go back and do it again, every single one of us would say, "Fuck yeah I would."

After all, it was The Road Less Travelled, and it ended up making all the difference in the world.

CHAPTER 16: GRUMPY

Weekends are a time for rest and relaxation. Well, at least on some other planet. In our house, if one or more of our kids didn't have a sports game or some other event to be at, then a niece, nephew or a friend's kid had a birthday party we were supposed to go to. Then, there were weddings – lots of them. It was always something, which sometimes made me a little grumpy, especially if I had other plans that weekend. There was also the possibility of the CRT team getting activated, which always happened at the worst possible time.

No matter what we had going on, I loved sitting down with the family to have an all-American style breakfast, with eggs, potatoes, bacon and toast. Breakfast has always been my favorite meal to sit down and eat, and I figured it was a nice break for the kids after eating cold cereal all week. When the kids were little, they loved helping with breakfast, which made it fun, but also a bit of a rodeo at times.

One particular morning, we were all making breakfast. Abigail was a baby and confined to a high chair, Walker was learning how to climb on things, Wyatt was learning to read and write, and Madeline was learning adolescent social skills.

The sound of eggs landing on the kitchen floor is always a distinct sound, especially when it is the sound of the entire dozen landing on the kitchen floor. Walker managed to scoot the chair over to the counter without me noticing, as I was preoccupied with potatoes cooking over here, bacon cooking over there, and so on and so forth. As the eggs hit the floor, I yelled out "Noooooooo!" as if I could stop it from happening. They didn't hit the floor at the same time, but more like *flap... flap-flap-flap... flap,* just to make it sound that much more unfortunate. As I stared down at the twelve eggs oozing all over the floor, Wyatt spoke up.

"You know, Dad, Walker knows how to stand on top of a chair now. You really need to watch him."

Then Madeline chimed in. "Yeah, Dad, you really need to watch him!"

Oh, okay, so it's *my* fault.

The thing about eggs is that it's always a good idea to have an extra dozen in the fridge. I had already learned that lesson. The other thing I learned about eggs is if you like them over medium, you have to pull them off the heat at just the right moment, because they will keep cooking for a few more minutes, and someone, I mean everyone, is going to remind you they like their eggs with runny yolks.

There were many lessons I learned over the years about bacon too. You have to watch bacon closely, and if you haven't tried cooking it in the oven, you don't know what you are missing. On a cookie sheet, over some aluminum foil, at 400 degrees, for 22 minutes or so, and it's easy-peasy. It didn't matter if it was eggs, bacon, toast, hash browns, or anything else involved with breakfast, I learned many tricks of the trade over the years. The best part was always when it was ready, and I'd set it all out on the table. As we dug in, it was not only the official commencement of our weekend, but also the official commencement of the family table banter.

"I don't want to go to school anymore," Madeline, who was nine years old at the time, announced matter-of-factly.

"Why?"

"*Ugh*, because there is this *boy* at school who is *bothering* us, and he is, like, just following us around."

"Well, I'm sorry," I said. "You have to go to school. It's like a law or something."

"But he is so *annoying*! *Ugh*!" She rolled her eyes and added, "I don't even like school anymore, because he won't leave us alone. I mean, we, like, *can't stand* him!"

"Just ignore him," I told her. "Plus, he's just one small person. Imagine working where I work, where there are a thousand people around you. I wish I had just one annoying person to have to deal with. That would be really cool."

"Dad, you don't even understand."

"Yes, I do."

"Alright, whatever, you two," Jody interrupts. "Everyone needs to finish eating and get cleaned up. We have to go to Stockton today."

"Seriously?" It shot out of my mouth uncontrollably, as I tossed my fork down on my plate. "Another birthday party?"

"Yes, another birthday party," Jody said. "You don't even have to be there, so don't get all grumpy about it."

A birthday party wasn't something that would normally stress me out, because I actually liked going to birthday parties. I just had plans that day. At the time, I had been feeling overwhelmed with everything going on, and I was planning to use that day to catch up on things around the yard. I had been spending a lot of time preparing for a two-week course coming up, and that was taking a lot of time. I was also coaching Madeline's softball team, so that was taking a lot of time. Add to that everything else that goes on when you have four children, including my commitment to the CRT team, and it left very little time left over. It was one of the reasons I enjoyed slowing down and having breakfast with the family. It gave us a chance to hang out together. Now, that was being rushed because we were supposed be going to a birthday party.

"Well, I'm going with you guys," I said. "And I am not grumpy. I just had a lot of stuff I wanted to do today."

"Well you don't have to go. Nobody wants you to go anyway, especially if you're grumpy."

"Okay, *now* I'm getting grumpy!"

"Dad," Wyatt interrupted. "How do you spell 'wunch'?"

"Wunch is not a word, buddy. You mean 'lunch,' right?" I start thinking to myself that we really don't have a lot of time for this.

"No, Dad, 'wunch.'"

"'Wunch' is not a word."

"Yes, it is, Dad! It *is* a word!"

"Okay, seriously, I went to college, and I'm sorry to tell you that 'wunch' is not a word. Are you sure you don't mean 'lunch'? As in l-u-n-c-h? Like what we eat in the afternoon? Wait a minute, why isn't Walker eating?"

"Dad, he isn't hungry," Wyatt said to me. He was not only Walker's older brother, but he was also his representative in all matters.

"What do you mean he isn't hungry? You guys have been complaining all morning because you were starving. How could he not be hungry?"

"He already ate some fruit snacks. And a cookie. And an apple. And, umm, some more fruit snacks."

"What!?"

"Yeah, Dad," Madeline chimed in. "You really need to start watching him." She didn't even look up from her plate.

"No. Stop. Everyone wait a minute!" I looked over at Walker and decided to bypass his representative. "Please tell me you didn't already eat."

He didn't say anything, but he kind of leant back a little and slyly peered under the table. I leant over and looked down at the floor. Underneath the table I saw an apple core, some cookie crumbs, and four empty fruit snack wrappers.

"What the…?"

"Dad, I told you this already. He is big enough to stand on a chair. You really need to…"

"Okay! Yes, I need to watch him. Got it."

"Dad, you still haven't told me how to spell 'wunch.'"

"It's not a word."

"Dad!"

"Okay, it's w-u-n-c-h! It's not a word, but it's W-U-N-C-H."

"Yeah, you're grumpy alright," Jody commented. "What's wrong with you, anyway?"

Everyone at the table stopped eating and looked up to wait for my answer.

"There is nothing wrong with me! I'm just thinking about all the stuff I have to do today that I can't do now."

"When was the last time you played the guitar?" Jody asked.

"What does that have to do with anything?"

"Well, you get grumpy when you haven't been playing the guitar."

"I haven't had time to play the guitar."

"Make time."

"And, Dad," Wyatt now interrupted. "'Wunch' IS a word." They might as well gang up on me now that I'm weakened.

"No, it is *not*."

"Yes, it IS!" He seemed really mad. He disappeared to his room and came out with his backpack. After digging around in it, he pulled out a sheet of paper, obviously homework from earlier in the week.

"Look, Dad, right HERE!" he pointed to the sheet. "I have to write 'wunch' with all the other ABCs!"

"Oh, you're practicing the alphabet," I realized. "Here, let me see it. I'll help you." I suddenly felt bad, thinking what kind of dad doesn't help his kid with the ABCs?

I looked at the sheet of paper and saw he had almost all of the letters written perfectly. It was down at the bottom of the sheet where I saw the problem. The ABCs do not stop at the letter Z. I should have known that.

At the bottom of the sheet he had written, "Now I know my ABCs, next time *wunch* you sing with me…"

On the way to the birthday party, I kept glancing into the rear-view mirror to check on Wyatt. He had a way of sometimes making a pouty face that wouldn't go away until you made it better. I wondered if I needed to say anything, or maybe just let the whole spelling thing go. He saw me looking at him and he smiled, letting me know all was well. I decided to say something anyways.

"Hey buddy."

"Yeah, Dad?"

"Just so you know, 'wunch' really is a word. You were right. It's a *great* word."

"I know Dad."

I told myself the first thing I would do when we got home was I'd play some guitar, no matter how much time I had. It was apparently a dog that really needed to be fed.

CHAPTER 17: MAKING A DIFFERENCE

Every class has its own feel. Some classes are full of comedians, as students one-up each other's jokes and make fun of each other. Some classes are more sarcastic, and you can hear them talking about how "fantastic" this class is probably going to be even before you walk into the room. Some classes are contemptuous, and students are either grumbling about having to be there or about life in general.

The toughest class to deal with is the one that is silent. That's the class that comes in, sits down, and then just stares at the front of the classroom waiting for something to happen. When it's that kind of class, you can't tell what they're thinking. If they make it obvious they hate being there, at least you know what you're dealing with.

A California Department of Corrections training classroom is a tough crowd. I can't imagine a more difficult group to win over. They're about as cynical as you will find, and it's understandable, considering anytime they gather for training, someone is telling them things have changed.

"Everyone, be advised there is a new policy, so disregard what you learned last time. We no longer do things that way."

Every year, the same thing.

"Who comes up with this shit?" they ask.

"Well, it's the same people who came up with last year's shit," the instructor tells them. "They're coming up with this new shit, so you can do your job better."

"But the people who came up with this new shit have never actually done my job," someone replies.

Hmm, good point. Be careful how you respond, because if you say the wrong thing, you will totally lose them. It's one thing to try to put a positive spin on things, but it's another thing to look like your trying to shine a turd. When you become an instructor, the last thing you want to do is look disingenuous or fake. A class, especially a department of corrections class, is already familiar with the new instructor who just came back from a trainer's course and now wants to change the world. They've already had the instructor who somehow thinks he has a trick up his sleeve other instructors before him didn't have.

When you agree to teach a class in the training room, you are putting yourself out there. Some of the students are going to take their shots at you, whether it is directly at you or under their breath to the person sitting next to them. Most of them will probably just sit there quietly and wait for it to be over. Sometimes, as you walk up to the front of the classroom and start your introduction, you realize nobody in that class gives one shit about what you're about to try to teach them. You dig in and try to grab their interest, but it's not a huge boost to your confidence when you see they are already glancing up at the clock. Go ahead, instructor, teach away. Let's see what you got.

Some instructors push too hard, and the class just shake their heads thinking, *Oh boy, here we go again*, *another one of* those *instructors*. Some instructors are meek and uninteresting, and the students end up taking control, coming and going as they please, tinkering on the computers, talking about last night's football game, or maybe under their breath about how much you suck as an instructor.

Most instructors lose interest in just a few months, because it sounds like a great idea, until you realize your teaching to a bunch of people who are forced to be there in class. Anyone can stand up there in front of the big whiteboard and rattle off from a lesson plan or read through a bunch of PowerPoint slides. Anyone can play a funny video, tell a war story, or conjure up classroom support by bad-mouthing the president, the government, the governor, the prison administration, the warden, the supervisors, or anyone else who is subject to criticism. The real challenge is making the uninteresting interesting. It's taking any subject and finding a way to get people to listen. If you can get up there with your own unique style and voice and get people interested in your how-to-be-a-better-prison-guard class, you've managed to do something you should be proud of, because it is not easy.

The training manager was responsible to oversee all formal training that took place for the officers. It was one of the more sought-after jobs if you were a lieutenant. Not only did it have weekends and holidays off, but you didn't have to work inside the prison walls, since the training department was outside the gate. I didn't really care about the days off or whether or not it was inside the gate. I just wanted to help officers become better officers.

When the warden called me into his office and offered me the position, I jumped in with both feet. The very first thing I did was to go and take the approved, mandated training agenda headquarters sent us and toss it in the trash. Every year, they would send out an agenda of state-mandated topics that we were required to follow for training, and each year we saw the amount of officer safety material get progressively less and less.

The schedule for officers' annual training seemed absurd to me, because it was more about the inmates than it was about the officers. It was based largely on court compliance issues and topics influenced by inmate lawsuits and rehabilitation mandates. The "officer" subjects, like handcuffing, self-defense, tactical decision-making, threat-level assessments and basic peace officer classes like "Laws of Arrest" or "Search and Seizure" were totally missing. I am on board with the idea that we should do what we can to help inmates leave the prison system better than when they arrived, but I didn't like the way the focus of our job became inmate medical care, rehabilitation programs and doing whatever it took to reduce prison sentences. It was frustrating to see how it overshadowed the needs of officers.

By that time, I'd already spent several years as a firearms, baton, and use of force instructor, and I had taught a lot of subjects related to SERT and CRT. I was excited to go into the training department, because I knew I'd have a chance to be more involved in what officers were learning.

The subject I was most involved in at that time was called "Alarm Response," which was the tactics officers used to quell prison riots. I was certified as a "master trainer" for Alarm Response, which is a fancy title that simply meant I was qualified to train the trainers. I was also certified as a "subject matter expert" in it, which resulted in me becoming the coordinator at our prison for our Alarm Response policy. That meant I wrote our plan and updated it annually, and I scheduled and supervised all of our Alarm Response training and drills.

My experience with Alarm Response also gave me the opportunity to be involved in the department's Reality-Based Alarm Response Instructor Course, and I assisted in developing the first of several courses and served as an instructor for them. I am very proud to have been involved in this, because those reality-based training courses changed the way officers dealt with violence in the prison system. Altogether, 30,000 correctional peace officers in the State of California would end up being trained in Alarm Response tactics so they could deal with the riots occurring at their prisons more effectively. The thing we were most proud of was the significant reduction in officer injuries, because officers had better tactics to utilize.

I had been the Alarm Response coordinator at our prison for the twelve years preceding my assignment to the training department. It was a difficult position to be in, because whenever there was a problem with the way officers responded to a riot, it became my responsibility to fix it. With six hundred correctional officers at the prison, that was a lot of people to reach when there was a training issue. The way I saw it, going into the training department would make it a lot easier for me to accomplish that task.

When I took over the training manager position, my goal was to make sure people in class had an opportunity to get something out of each class. I tried to think outside the box. I spent a lot of time coming up with different ways to get through to people, and that became my teaching style. I knew going at them straight ahead, by simply regurgitating the lesson plan or telling them "You have to know this, because it's your JOB to know it!" – like some instructors did – wasn't going to cut it. I wanted to be better than that.

I had fun coming up with different material for the different classes I taught, because I wanted to make things interesting. I had learned from some of the more effective instructors I knew that you had to make it entertaining if you wanted them to listen. I put together presentations on topics like the Hundred Years' War in the 1300s between France and England, as well as other historical events, and I presented them like a history lesson in a college course rather than as a mandatory training class for work. I'd then try to use that information to lead into the subject I was teaching by finding a nexus between them. I researched, found photos, drew maps and even recited Shakespeare if I had to, just to change things up.

I also started writing articles for our training bulletin, which was the monthly publication we put out for the employees at the prison. I wanted to write something for people to enjoy reading each month, and I didn't want it to be too serious or too much about work. I knew having four small kids would provide plenty of entertaining material, so I used some of the things that happened at home as anecdotes, and I tried to relate them to life at work. I underestimated how many people at work would actually read those articles.

It wasn't always positive though. One day, an officer stopped me in the hallway and asked why I put my personal life in the bulletin. I told him I was trying to change things up in the training department, and I wanted to give people something positive to read. He thought it was waste of time. I told him that I figured people could related to my stories, and with all the seriousness going on a little levity might go a long way. He shook his head and walked away. I was pretty sure he wasn't the only one who was critical of the articles.

Not long after that, I began realizing how writing articles every month was putting too much on my plate, because of the amount of time they were taking. I also thought about how some people were probably just scoffing at the articles rather than seeing them as a positive. I decided to stop writing them.

I immediately started receiving phone calls and emails. Employees were stopping me in the parking lot to ask what happened to the articles. The head of our education department stood up during one of our morning managers' meetings and announced how much he and his employees enjoyed and appreciated my articles. Wow, even the head of our EDUCATION department! I realized we don't often get this kind of reward in our line of work, so I kept writing the articles.

At that time, Jody worked third watch, so we didn't have to rely on people to watch the kids. With her on third watch and me on second watch, there would always be at least one of us at home. It was a bit crazy, though. As I was driving home, and she was driving to work, we'd sometimes wave as we saw each other out on the highway. She also arranged her schedule by swapping work shifts with people, so she could have the weekends off.

Working the swaps meant she worked a "double" from 1430 to 0630 hours twice a week, which meant she went to work in the afternoon and didn't get home until the morning. With that schedule, she took care of the morning things like getting the kids dressed and taking them to school, and I took care of the evening things like picking them up from school, doing homework, taking them to practice, etc. As hectic as it was during the week, it was nice to not have to rely on people to watch our kids. If we ever needed a babysitter, it would only be for an hour or so, just to cover things until I got home. Then, with Jody's shift swaps, we were able to spend the entire weekend together as a family.

Every day after work, I'd pick up the kids from school on the way home. As soon as we walked into the house, I'd get into my workout clothes and try to get some workout in, usually right there in the living room, either doing a deck of cards workout or by putting on a workout DVD. I even started tossing in some yoga, just to help with the stress.

As I was working out, the kids would be running around the house doing what kids do, arguing, causing havoc and all other sorts of disorder. After my workout, if any possible combination of our children had wrestling, baseball, softball, soccer, or any other sport that day, I found a way to get them to it. Then, I'd figure out what was for dinner, followed by homework, followed by shower, followed by jammies, followed by trying to stop the kids from running all over the house.

If by then it wasn't time for bed, the kids and I might catch something on TV. We probably watched the movie *Jaws* a hundred times, but if there was a Giants game on TV, it was mandatory. I thought it was pretty cool how my kids knew the numbers of all the Giants players (which diminished once they discovered video games, sadly).

As bedtime approached, we'd all get down on our knees to say nighttime prayers, and after they stopped farting around and coming up with excuses to get out of their beds, they'd eventually fall asleep. Sometimes I'd walk back into their rooms to check on them after they fell asleep, and I'd regret how fast the day went by. I was right there with them, yet it felt like I somehow missed it all because we were in such a hurry. I'd even have the urge to wake them, because I wanted to hear their little voices.

Of course, I never woke them, though. I'd just walk back out to the couch to catch the rest of the game. Once in a while, but not often enough, I'd grab my guitar for a few minutes. If there was a CRT course coming up or a new class for In-Service Training, I'd reach over and grab my laptop to work on some classroom presentations, until I fell asleep in the chair. There were times when I'd wake up in that chair, and the game would be over, and I'd find my laptop still sitting there with the latest class presentation on the screen. Even at the end of the night, when I should have been relaxing, I was still working – that's how badly I wanted to make a difference.

CHAPTER 18: NEMESIS

However much I loved my work, over time the cynicism and negativity in our department started to have an effect on me. When you're writing the bulletin articles, and you're up there teaching the classes, and you're preaching that people should become better officers and they should take more pride in their jobs, you have to accept the fact that not everyone is going to like it. Some people will even try to knock you down a notch, and it is just the nature of the beast. I even had a fellow lieutenant make sure to stop by my office to let me know I was only fooling myself. He said officers cared more about what was in their lunch box than my Alarm Response plan. "Nobody really cares," he said.

Because of comments like that, I sometimes wondered if the effort was really worth it. I felt like it would be a lot easier if I didn't care. Having the opportunity to see every officer who worked at our prison, since they all had to show up for training, I had firsthand experience regarding how they felt about their job. Many of them were tired of feeling underappreciated by policy-makers who seemed preoccupied with their own career advancement. There was also an overwhelming amount of distrust for management, because of the subtle way officers were made to feel replaceable. Some of the officers saw me as being not much different than a manager. To some of them, I was no longer one of them, especially when you consider I was running my own department now, had an office, with a desk, and I had weekends and holidays off. It felt like I was surrounded by a thick cloud of cynicism that would never dissipate. One day, I was so fed up, I went back to my desk after a class and put my head in my hands. I wondered what I was doing to myself.

I looked over at my sergeant in the office, and I told him I was done. There would be no more planning out the classes, no more history lessons, no more stories, no more nexuses, no more nothing. I was tired of feeling like the only thing I was accomplishing was that I was just making myself out to be a pain in the ass. I was now going to give the stupid classes by using the stupid lesson plans exactly as they were written, and then I was going to have the officers just sign the stupid sign-in sheets to get credit for the stupid class. No more extra, no more drama.

My sergeant was not only a good sergeant, but he was also a good friend. He leaned back in his chair and calmly looked across the office at me.

"If you quit trying, then nothing will change. If you don't try to make a difference, who's gonna do it? Think about every single person you know who has ever made a difference. They were a pain in the ass."

I took some time to think about what he said, and I realized he was absolutely right. You cannot expect everyone to like and appreciate what you are doing, because that is a fool's game. You have to do it, because it is the right thing to do, and then you have to accept there will be obstacles. It doesn't mean you should stop fighting to make a difference.

At that point, I knew I was expecting too much from myself and I needed to cut myself some slack. I was trying too hard, because I wanted work to matter. I wanted it to mean something. Ultimately though, I had to accept the fact that some people won't like my ideas, and that meant tempering my expectations and getting my ego out of the way. It was at that point that I truly started to come into my own as an instructor. Although I was a *decent* instructor before, I became an *effective* instructor after. I also had to accept that it was perfectly ok to be a pain in the ass. Someone had to be one.

I realized teaching was more rewarding, and much more effective, when you let the students make up their own minds. All the hard work in the world isn't going to cause them to change. They have to change, because *they* want to do it. It has to be *their* idea. Show them why it's important to them, and demonstrate what benefits are possible from it, and then trust they are smart enough to decide for themselves. Don't try to force them. Once they are on-board, it is simply a matter of coaching them from that point forward, by standing back, observing, and then addressing one small correction at a time - it doesn't matter if you are teaching them how to respond to a riot, how to shoot a gun, or how to hit a curveball. The thing you have to remember is this: just because it is important to you, does not mean it is important to them. It has to be important to them. That was a valuable lesson I had to learn.

As I began adapting that way of thinking into my style of teaching, I started to get through to people. I continued the use of analogies and other examples to get my point across, but the difference was I tried to make sure the instruction was more about *them,* the students. I also realized obstacles were normal, and I learned to show students that I understood their obstacles, no matter if they were physical obstacles (they had trouble performing), or mental ones (they had trouble believing). Showing people I understood things from their perspective made me a much more effective instructor, because instead of taking it personally if I couldn't get through to someone, I accepted the fact that everyone has their own opinions and preferences.

I also started teaching at our CRT certification courses, where I'd become one of the primary, state-wide instructors for our CRT program. I would end up teaching officers from every prison in the state, and I had become fairly recognized within the 19 CRT teams across the state. Many of those officers often contacted me to tell me how much they enjoyed my teaching style, and how I had a way of explaining things in a way that made things simple. It meant a lot to me when they told me I influenced them to become better instructors back at their prisons.

Back at the training department, officers began stopping by my office to share information they had on some of the topics I brought up. Some of those officers who stopped by my office to compliment me were the most negative people I knew, and now, there they were, bringing in DVDs or books to share with me. I couldn't help but to feel like I had finally figured things out in my career. I felt like I had found my niche. It was a really good feeling to go into work each morning knowing I had something to offer. It was the first time in my career, outside of SERT and CRT, that I actually felt appreciated.

It was around that time that I got called to the chief deputy warden's office. The warden who hired me for the job had retired. When I walked into the office, it was immediately obvious I wasn't going to like the news I was getting.

He told me another lieutenant had complained because it wasn't fair that I had been in such a desired position for so long. Did one of my fellow lieutenants really walk into the warden's office to whine because things weren't "fair"? I wanted to vomit.

If the warden actually had any idea what I had just gone through for that job, our conversation would have been totally different. If he understood the lack of sleep, the personal time I invested, and the big, fat target I put upon myself by standing out there in front of his officers, trying to motivate them to do better, maybe it would have went down a little differently. Maybe I wouldn't have felt so expendable, replaceable, and like just the next number in line. Maybe instead of, "One of your peers is complaining because it's not really fair, so..." I could have gotten a "Thank you," which I never heard. Neither from him nor any other manager for that matter.

Maybe it wasn't his or anyone else's prerogative to care about how I felt or what I put into the job. I didn't expect him to try to make me feel better about it, but maybe it would have been nice to know someone appreciated the fucking rollercoaster I had gone through trying to make a difference. That's all.

So, just like that, I was done in that position. I tried to not take it personally, because it felt foolish to do so. Here's the thing, though: my entire career was something I took personally. After all, when I showed up at this old, decaying prison up in the hills, I somehow actually found a way to love my job, by helping others. If nothing else, it helped me make sense out of giving up my childhood and adolescent dreams, because helping people became something I believed in, and it was something I spent a ridiculous amount of my time and energy trying to get better at. It felt as if none of that really mattered much, because being replaced was out of my control, and it was apparently what was "fair" to someone else. So, yeah, I definitely took it personally. Very personally.

That job was never mine. It was only a position I was filling temporarily, just as all positions are filled temporarily. You're holding it until the next person takes over, and then they hold it until the next one in line takes over, and so on and so forth. Maybe that's why some people choose to simply get by in their positions and do the minimum – they know that it's not going to make much difference in the long run. Management doesn't really mind, because everyone is replaceable, and it's never personal to them, because it is happening to someone *else*.

There I was, standing in front of all those officers, giving those classes, trying to find ways to encourage officers to try harder, and to overcome the stereotypes people had of them. I wanted to change the way they saw their jobs, and for them to be more committed, yet in the end I became the perfect example of why so many of them would never chose to do so.

The internal struggle I felt to justify the path I took in life became a dilemma that would shadow my entire career. More than an affliction, it became my nemesis, always present, causing uncertainty, and making me question what kind of person I was supposed to be. I now realize it was unfair to make myself struggle with such a thing, considering no single job could possibly define who it is that we are supposed to be. After all, we are who we are. Although I spent twenty-three years working in a prison, I realize am not a correctional officer. I am so much more than that.

Was it possible to ever fall in love my job? Could I do enough to make such a thing happen? I don't know, but it is amazing how much good came to my life because of the job. My wife. My kids. All the best friends, great friends and good friends I made. My SERT/CRT involvement, where I had the opportunity to influence so many people, and where I met some of the most honest, hardworking and talented people you could ever imagine. Because of that job, I made the most amazing friendships, from Pelican Bay up north, all the way down south to Centinela State Prison down south. And it is because of all those wonderful things I got out of my career that I do not regret taking the job, not for one single moment. What I can't do, though, is tell myself I'd do it again.

I found out it was possible to do this job and not become some mindless knuckle dragger like some movies portray officers to be. Even when you find yourself surrounded by so much negativity, you can still enjoy your job if you find a way to do in in your own way, and with your own personality. You don't have to be like anyone else. Again, your job does not define who you are supposed to be.

I thought back to the most important lessons I learned over my life, whether they were as a child, soldier, student, parent, or a twenty-three year correctional officer. If there was nothing else I learned from those experiences, I learned that challenges will come, and they will go. Before I knew it, instead of being upset about my job, I felt a calm sense of acceptance about it. I knew that I would never be able to defeat my own personal nemesis. After all, no matter where it is I go, or what it is I do, I will always feel caught between two extremes: The guy who fights bad guys, or the guy who plays guitar solos. Experience has taught me that no matter which side I fed more, I could not do either one halfway. Something tells me I would have gone through the same type of dilemma no matter which career path I took.

CHAPTER 19: OLD SCHOOL

A lieutenant used to be a big deal. They ran the show. I remember the old school lieutenants when I was a new officer, and how they had a way about them. They were definitely not the people you wanted to piss off, and it didn't matter if you were an inmate, an officer, or their management. They had the answers, and if you went to them with a problem, they knew how to fix it. They also knew how to get you out of trouble.

Back when I first promoted to lieutenant, it didn't take long for me to understand why some of those old school lieutenants were the way they were. As a lieutenant, if you wanted to get your job done, you didn't have a whole lot of time to put up with unnecessary bullshit, and it didn't matter if it was coming from the inmates, your subordinates, or your management. I never purposely set out to be like some of those lieutenants, but as I found myself having more of an interest in principle than in politesse, it made me appreciate the way some of them went about their job.

Maybe that was why some of the younger guys sometimes called me old school, or OG. I even got a "Double OG" on occasion. It had to do with my experience and time in the department, but I think also with the fact that I didn't let the pressures of the job change my priorities. I never thought of myself as being an OG, because I never thought of myself as being old enough to be OG. Plus, there was always a bit of immaturity in me that I hid from those who did not know me. The truth was, I actually kind of saw myself as a nerd who still watched Star Wars and snickered at words like *butthole*. Nevertheless, I appreciated the compliment, because an OG was someone you respected because they never did things to impress anyone - they just tried to do the right thing.

I always wanted to be approachable. I enjoyed it when people stopped by my office to talk about any subject, no matter if it was sports, hunting, music, golf or even fantasy football. I was never shy or hesitant about taking charge of things when I ran a yard, especially if we had an incident, and I hoped people saw past the lieutenant bars on my collar and took me for the person I really was. In terms of appearance, I always tried to look professional. I wore a formal, pressed uniform, with a tie, every day, but it was never because I wanted to be treated formally. Most of the officers called me by my first name, and that was how I preferred things to be. It felt uncomfortable when officers called me "Lieutenant" because it made things too official.

Although we were never on a first name basis, it was also important for me to have a mutual respect with the inmates. My methods for dealing with inmates evolved over the years, and I must admit that I cringe when I sometimes think back to my younger, more hot-headed ways. I used to think you had to show inmates you were not intimidated by them, and that you were willing to stand your ground. Although it certainly would do you no good to walk around being afraid of inmates, those who camouflaged it with false bravado only caused themselves more problems.

As a new and inexperienced officer, there were many times during my drive home after work where I cursed myself the whole way home, because I was so upset for letting some inmate get under my skin. I eventually realized it never actually gives you much satisfaction to get back at an inmate, and if you go around taking things too personally, there is just going to be another inmate to get back at next time, and then another one after that, and on and on. It would never end.

Once I became a lieutenant, I really got to see how some officers brought certain problems upon themselves because of the way they dealt with inmates. I was extremely protective of my officers, but at the same time I was honest with them if I thought they were wrong. Since I had been in their shoes, I knew what it was like to allow emotions to get the best of me, and even after promoting to sergeant, and then lieutenant, you are certainly not immune to it. Some inmates are very difficult to deal with, especially in areas like the lockup unit where inmates could spend the entire eight-hour shift berating you from behind their cell door. Some of them had the ability to come up with the most horrible things a person could possibly to say to another human being, and it was often the female staff who got the worst of it. They were things nobody should ever have to listen to. It's easy to say they are just words, until you've had to hear it for eight hours straight.

As difficult as some situations were to deal with, I understood that not all inmates were like that, and if you were respectful and just trying to do your time, then I treated you like a person rather than an inmate. In fact, if an inmate was in the right, I would not hesitate to speak up for him. Without a doubt, I enforced an expectation that inmates in my area follow the rules and were respectful to the officers, but at the same time, that standard also applied to the officers in my area. I didn't care if you were an officer or an inmate, if you caused problems, I had no problem addressing it. I wasn't one to use formal paperwork to speak for me, like some preferred to use, and I wouldn't allow administrators to pressure me to write someone up. I preferred to give someone a chance to hear me out, and then, even if they didn't like what I had to say, they had a chance to vent behind closed doors. That was sometimes all someone needed – to be heard and to get it off their chest.

There was a time when it wasn't good if you had to go see the lieutenant. It meant you must have really screwed up, and the situation was beyond what the sergeant could mitigate. When the lieutenant brought you into their office back then, you kept your mouth shut and listened if you were smart, because he was probably going to save your ass. However, they also had the ability to give you an ass-chewing you would never forget. This newer generation does not deal with ass-chewings very well, so you have to know how to talk to everyone who works for you. Each employee requires a different approach, and it's just one more good reason why your employees shouldn't be treated like a number.

When I was new to the department, officers had a lot of respect for their lieutenants. They usually went to their lieutenant because they trusted them. Things seem different now, and I am not sure why that is. Maybe some of it has to do with this being a different kind of generation. Maybe some of it has to do with lieutenants walking around with a beard that circumvents the grooming standards. Whatever it is, a lieutenant doesn't seem to be as big of a deal any more.

That definitely contributed to my decision to leave the department. I understood the fact that things change over time, but it was getting to where I was no longer recognizing the department I once thought I knew. There was so much retirement taking place in high-ranking positions that it created a huge potential for upward mobility. As a result of so many interested applicants jockeying for position, we saw the pressure it put on people to micromanage everyone else below them, not only while they were in acting positions, but also after they were hired for the position. They were staying late, sending paperwork back for ridiculous corrections, and they were allowing us to make fewer and fewer decisions without first getting their approval. While a lieutenant used to be someone who ran their own yard, it suddenly felt like nobody trusted them to make a decision. You were no longer paid to utilize discretion. It's not much fun to work in a place like that.

I spent more time in my career being responsible for other people than not being responsible for people. It all started when I became the company commander of Sierra Company at the correctional officer academy. From that point forward, I seemed to find myself in positions where I was supervising or training people. I always took those roles very seriously, because I never wanted to let people down.

Sometimes leading people was easy, while other times it was hard. I had to learn it on my own, because the department doesn't teach you how to do it. It doesn't even give you an example, because it tends to manage rather than lead. Most lessons I learned about leadership over my career were learned the hard way, by doing things wrong and then later driving home from work swearing I would never repeat that mistake.

Even if there were times I did not like my job, I always enjoyed being a supervisor, because of how good it felt to help people. I especially loved being the CRT commander though, because I felt like a father looking over my own children. That is how much I cared and looked out for my guys, and how much I enjoyed watching them grow. They meant so much more to me than they ever realized. There were times they probably didn't understand my decisions, but something tells me one day they will, especially as they move into leadership roles of their own.

I ended up serving our SERT/CRT program for over twenty-one years out of my twenty-three year career. The most fulfilling aspect of my career was being able to retire from the department and from CRT the same day. When I stepped into my pickup truck and drove away from the prison that last day, it would also be the day I left CRT. That was very special to me, because after all, going back to that day I was lying on my back doing sit-ups with a log over my chest, it was something I could not quit.

I never hesitated to do whatever it took for the guys on my team, and political correctness, upward mobility, and even common sense never stopped me from defending them. If you screwed with my guys, you would have to deal with me. In fact, there were several notable times in my career when this spoiled my relationships with people. The bottom line was this: don't mess with my guys, no matter who you are. Going back to what I learned from First Sergeant Stanley back in the Army, there was no other option but to go to the mat for any one of your guys. That might be called "old school" to some. Maybe it is considered "inadvisable" to others. It probably depends on how important upward mobility is to you. Whatever you want to call it, I'm very proud that was how I went about my job, every single day. It was how the OG's once did it, which meant it was good enough for me.

EPILOGUE

Once in a while, I am reminded of how much that job changed me. There are parts of me that will never be the same, and I don't mean that as necessarily a good thing or a bad thing. For example, I now keep a careful, focused eye on people everywhere I go. I look at tattoos, because I know there is a difference between prison tattoos and those that aren't. Even black tattoos from a tattoo parlor don't have that same look, when you've spent any time behind the walls of a prison. Not that tattoos are a bad thing, but they tend to indicate when people are proud of their criminal lifestyle. It's good to know who those people are.

I also sit in restaurants where I can watch people come and go. People who look out of place make me nervous. I pay attention to things I never really cared about before. Over my career, I learned too much about humans and about the evil that exists in the world. I sometimes have trouble letting my kids be kids, because if I can't see where they are or who is around them, I get nervous. I'm getting better with that, as each passing day leads me to be less and less uptight. I am happier and nicer now, and I seem to have left my "focus face" at the prison when I walked out that last time.

I always wondered what I'd do on my first day after leaving the department. I thought about going up over the pass in the mountains and finding a trail to run on. Maybe I'd find a scenic spot overlooking the trees, and do some pushups, burpees and dive-bombers. Then I thought, *Nah, what the hell would I need to do something like that for?*

As it turns out, the first thing I did on that first morning was to wake up, grab a cup of coffee and sit out on my porch with my guitar in my hands. I figured the first day of the rest of my life should be spent doing something I really loved.

It became my morning ritual. My morning guitar practice routine would usually take two cups of coffee, three on a really good day, until it was time to wake up the kids for school. Once the kids were up and their beds were made, I'd do Abigail's hair. It wouldn't take long before I got really good at it. It became our thing. Sometimes, I'd even sing to her *Farewell and Adieu.*

I always told Jody that whenever I left the department, I wanted to take the kids on a road trip. I wanted to know what it was like to spend quality time with my family without wondering when my phone was going to ring from work. So, we packed up the fifth wheel and took off. It would end up being an amazing 5,000-mile trip to Yellowstone, Mt. Rushmore and through many of the western states. It was completely therapeutic; spending that kind of quality time with my family was priceless.

While we were on that trip, I got a call from someone who had retired from the prison several years before. Coincidentally, he was also a SERT member before my time on the team. He called to say he was in a blues/classic rock band, and they were looking for a lead guitarist. As it turns out, I did get a phone call on our trip, except it was a different kind of work.

And now, here I am, out of the department and in a band. Playing music now is much different than any other time in my life, because I'm no longer wondering if I should chase my dream to play music or if I should find a good job. It is not a dilemma in my life anymore.

My job was rewarding because of the emotional connections I had with people. I met a lot of people in that job over the years, including officers, supervisors, managers, and even inmates. When I left the department, it meant a lot to me when people stopped by my office to tell me they appreciated how I had somehow influenced them. This included inmates too, who either stopped by to talk to me before I left or dropped a letter off on my desk to thank me for being the type of lieutenant that I was. I appreciated that, because that was something they didn't have to do, but it felt good to know someone out there appreciated the way I went about my job. Over my career I didn't always get that, if this book hasn't already made that clear. It made me realize the most important part of our job is how we chose to treat people.

Experience and maturity have taught me whatever path you think you are supposed to take when you are younger will probably differ from the one you end up taking. Last-minute, unexpected turns are important parts of life, and you have to make the best of them. We constantly look for verification that we have made the right choices in life. As long as you treat people with dignity, stay true to who you are, and no matter what else, always try to do the right thing, you will be proud of whatever path you take. I really hope my children take this to heart when they face the various paths in their own lives.

In life, it is not what you do, but how you do it. If you have a passion in life, find a way to do it. No matter if it is playing music, painting, rock climbing, or whatever, if you ignore the voice in your heart, you will always wonder what would have been. Don't listen to anyone else.

Don't forget that no matter what it is that you choose to do with your life, it is *not* your job that defines who you are. Don't wait until you retire to make time for whatever it is you love to do. Do what you love. Keep your passion in your life. Don't ever expect you'll outgrow it, because you won't.

Made in the USA
San Bernardino, CA
16 September 2019